The Byzantine Empire

Titles in the World History Series

WORLD HISTORY SERIES ■ ■ ■

The Byzantine Empire

by
James A. Corrick

Lucent Books, P.O. Box 289011, San Diego, CA 92198-9011

*For Thomas B. Costain, Rafael Sabatini, and Samuel Shellabarger,
through whose novels I discovered that history could
entertain as well as enlighten*

Library of Congress Cataloging-in-Publication Data

Corrick, James A.
    The Byzantine Empire / by James A. Corrick.
        p. cm.—(World history series)
    Includes bibliographical references and index.
    Summary: A historical overview of the cultural
phenomenon of the Byzantine Empire and its legacy.
    ISBN 1-56006-307-6 (alk. paper)
    1. Byzantine Empire—Civilization—Juvenile literature.
[1. Byzantine Empire—Civilization.]   I. Title.   II. Series.
DF552.C67   1997
949.5—dc20
                                                    96-34600
                                                       CIP
                                                        AC

Copyright 1997 by Lucent Books, Inc., P.O. Box 289011,
San Diego, California 92198-9011

Printed in the U.S.A.

Contents

Foreword

Each year on the first day of school, nearly every history teacher faces the task of explaining why his or her students should study history. One logical answer to this question is that exploring what happened in our past explains how the things we often take for granted—our customs, ideas, and institutions—came to be. As statesman and historian Winston Churchill put it, "Every nation or group of nations has its own tale to tell. Knowledge of the trials and struggles is necessary to all who would comprehend the problems, perils, challenges, and opportunities which confront us today." Thus, a study of history puts modern ideas and institutions in perspective. For example, though the founders of the United States were talented and creative thinkers, they clearly did not invent the concept of democracy. Instead, they adapted some democratic ideas that had originated in ancient Greece and with which the Romans, the British, and others had experimented. An exploration of these cultures, then, reveals their very real connection to us through institutions that continue to shape our daily lives.

Another reason often given for studying history is the idea that lessons exist in the past from which contemporary societies can benefit and learn. This idea, although controversial, has always been an intriguing one for historians. Those that agree that society can benefit from the past often quote philosopher George Santayana's famous statement, "Those who cannot remember the past are condemned to repeat it." Historians who ascribe to Santayana's philosophy believe that, for example, studying the events that led up to the major world wars or other significant historical events would allow society to chart a different and more favorable course in the future.

Just as difficult as convincing students to realize the importance of studying history is the search for useful and interesting supplementary materials that present historical events in a context that can be easily understood. The volumes in Lucent Books' World History Series attempt to present a broad, balanced, and penetrating view of the march of history. Ancient Egypt's important wars and rulers, for example, are presented against the rich and colorful backdrop of Egyptian religious, social, and cultural developments. The series engages the reader by enhancing historical events with these cultural contexts. For example, in *Ancient Greece*, the text covers the role of women in that society. Slavery is discussed in *The Roman Empire*, as well as how slaves earned their freedom. The numerous and varied aspects of everyday life in these and other societies are explored in each volume of the series. Additionally, the series covers the major political, cultural, and philosophical ideas as the torch of civilization is passed from ancient Mesopotamia and Egypt, through Greece, Rome, Medieval Europe, and other world cultures, to the modern day.

The material in the series is formatted in a thorough, precise, and organized manner. Each volume offers the reader a comprehensive and clearly written overview of an important historical event or period. The topic under discussion is placed in a broad historical context. For example, *The Italian Renaissance* begins with a discussion of the High Middle Ages and the loss of central control that allowed certain Italian cities to develop artistically. The book ends by looking forward to the Reformation and interpreting the societal changes that grew out of the Renaissance. Thus, students are not only involved in an historical era, but also enveloped by the events leading up to that era and the events following it.

One important and unique feature in the World History Series is the primary and secondary source quotations that richly supplement each volume. These quotes are useful in a number of ways. First, they allow students access to sources they would not normally be exposed to because of the difficulty and obscurity of the original source. The quotations range from interesting anecdotes to farsighted cultural perspectives and are drawn from historical witnesses both past and present. Second, the quotes demonstrate how and where historians themselves derive their information on the past as they strive to reach a consensus on historical events. Lastly, all of the quotes are footnoted, familiarizing students with the citation process and allowing them to verify quotes and/or look up the original source if the quote piques their interest.

Finally, the books in the World History Series provide a detailed launching point for further research. Each book contains a bibliography specifically geared toward student research. A second, annotated bibliography introduces students to all the sources the author consulted when compiling the book. A chronology of important dates gives students an overview, at a glance, of the topic covered. Where applicable, a glossary of terms is included.

In short, the series is designed not only to acquaint readers with the basics of history, but also to make them aware that their lives are a part of an ongoing human saga. Perhaps they will then come to the same realization as famed historian Arnold Toynbee. In his monumental work, *A Study of History*, he wrote about becoming aware of history flowing through him in a mighty current, and of his own life "welling like a wave in the flow of this vast tide."

Important Dates in the History of the Byzantine Empire

A.D.	330	400	450	500	550	600	650	700	750	800	850

A.D.

330
Roman emperor Constantine I founds Constantinople and makes it the capital of the Roman Empire.

364
Roman emperor Valentinian I divides the empire into western and eastern segments; Valens becomes the first eastern emperor, with his capital at Constantinople.

378
The Visigoths defeat a Roman army at Adrianople and kill the eastern emperor Valens.

410
The Visigoths sack the city of Rome.

451
The Council of Chalcedon proclaims Monophysitism a heresy.

476
The barbarian Odovacar deposes the western emperor Romulus Augustulus and becomes the ruler of Italy; the eastern Roman Empire is now the Byzantine Empire.

493
The Ostrogoths, led by Theodoric, invade Italy and kill Odovacar.

527
Justinian I and Theodora become emperor and empress.

529
Codex Justinianus, the Code of Justinian, replaces the old Byzantine legal code.

532
The Nika riot erupts in Constantinople.

533
Belisarius conquers North Africa.

536
Belisarius invades the Ostrogothic kingdom in Italy and captures Rome.

537
The Church of Santa Sophia in Constantinople is completed.

540
Belisarius captures Ravenna, the Ostrogothic capital.

550
The Slavs enter the Balkans.

552
The Byzantine general Narses drives the Ostrogoths out of Italy.

554
The empire reaches its greatest extent.

568
The Lombards begin conquering northern Italy.

582
Combined Avar-Slav armies invade the empire's Balkan holdings.

602
The emperor Maurice is overthrown, and Persia attacks the empire, eventually capturing the Near Eastern provinces, as well as Egypt.

610
Heraclius becomes emperor.

622
Heraclius takes the offensive against Persia.

626
Constantinople survives a siege by both the Avars and the Persians.

629
Heraclius defeats the Persians and recovers lost Byzantine territory.

635
Arab Muslims conquer Syria.

637
The Arabs take Jerusalem.

641
Egypt and Persia fall to the Arabs.

674
An Arab fleet unsuccessfully attacks Constantinople.

680
The Bulgars enter the Balkans and establish a kingdom.

698
The Arabs conquer North Africa.

717
Leo III becomes emperor and defeats a large Muslim army and navy at Constantinople.

726
Iconoclasm begins in the empire.

811
The Bulgars defeat a Byzantine army and kill the emperor, Nicephorus I.

843
Church council ruling ends official support for iconoclasm.

863–864
Slavs begin converting to Christianity.

867
Basil I becomes the first Macedonian emperor.

893
Symeon establishes the Bulgarian Empire.

989
Russia joins the Byzantine church.

996
Emperor Basil II passes laws to curb the Powerful.

1025
Upon the death of Basil II, his restrictions upon the Powerful are lifted.

1054
The western and eastern branches of the church permanently separate.

1071
The empire loses Bari, its last outpost in Italy, to the Normans and loses the Battle of Manzikert and much of Asia Minor to the Seljuk Turks.

1081–1082
Alexius I becomes emperor; Venice is given special trading rights with the empire.

1095–1099
Pope Urban II calls for the First Crusade; crusaders take Jerusalem and found the crusader states.

1171
Emperor Manuel I cancels Venice's trading rights within the empire.

1182
Thousands of western Europeans are massacred in Constantinople.

1185
Normans plunder Thessalonica; the Venetians regain imperial trading rights.

1187
The Muslims recapture Jerusalem.

1204–1205
The Fourth Crusade sacks Constantinople and sets up the Latin Empire; Emperor Theodore Lascaris establishes a Byzantine government in exile at Nicaea.

1214
War between the Latin Empire and the Nicaean Empire ends in a stalemate.

1259–1261
Michael VIII becomes emperor of Nicaea; he and his army recapture Constantinople, ending the Latin Empire and restoring the Byzantine.

1354
The Ottoman Turks occupy Gallipoli.

1363
The Ottomans move their capital from Asia Minor to Adrianople.

1449
The last Byzantine emperor, Constantine XI, assumes his post.

1453
Led by Mehmet II, the Ottoman Turks capture Constantinople, killing Constantine XI and ending the Byzantine Empire.

The Legacy of Empire

In A.D. 476, the Roman emperor Romulus Augustulus (Romulus, the little Augustus) was overthrown, and the first in a series of non-Roman kings took his place, thus marking the end of the Roman Empire. However, this imperial collapse affected only the western half of the empire. The eastern part, under its own emperor, survived for another thousand years. This eastern Roman Empire would be known to later historians as the Byzantine Empire.

The Byzantine Empire, which did not fall until 1453, when the Ottoman Turks overran it, spanned the Middle Ages, the period of European history that lasted from about 500 to approximately 1500. During much of the empire's long existence, it was the major European power. While barbarian warlords fought and struggled to create kingdoms out of the shattered western Roman Empire, the Byzantine Empire flourished, remaining a center for art and learning.

The Classical Empire

Throughout their entire history, the Byzantines called themselves Romans because they always thought of their realm as the Roman Empire. In the same spirit, the Byzantine emperors believed that they were the direct heirs of the emperors of Rome. Yet, to the kingdoms of western Europe, the empire was Greek, and indeed, by the seventh century A.D., the official language of the Byzantines was Greek, not Latin. The label "Byzantine" was the creation of post-Renaissance historians and was not used by the Byzantines themselves.

The Byzantine Empire's fifth-century territory included the Balkan peninsula, Asia Minor, the Near East, and Egypt. Its capital was Constantinople, named for the Roman emperor Constantine I, who built the city on an earlier Greek settlement in the fourth century A.D. The city, as well as the entire empire, was also known as Byzantium, from the name of the original Greek town's legendary founder, Byzas.

Constantinople sat on the European side of the Bosporus, the narrow northernmost section of the Straits, the well-known waterway that also includes the Sea of Marmara and the Dardanelles. The Straits link the Black Sea to the Aegean Sea, part of the Mediterranean. They also divide Europe from Asia. The Byzantine capital was perfectly positioned to control trade moving north and south through the Straits and east and west across the Bosporus.

Throughout the Middle Ages, Constantinople was called simply the City. Its

Roman emperor Constantine I built Constantinople in the fourth century A.D. Ideally located to control trade in the area, Constantinople became the thriving capital of the Byzantine Empire.

modern name, Istanbul, is nothing but a distortion of the Greek phrase "to the city." In size and population, Constantinople was like a modern city. The rest of Europe had nothing that could rival it. Even the city of Rome had only a fraction of the population and splendor of the eastern capital. Historian Will Durant remarks that within a century of Constantinople's construction:

> It contained . . . almost a million [people]. An official document . . . lists five imperial palaces, six palaces for the ladies of the court, three for

high dignitaries, 4,388 mansions, 322 streets, . . . [and one must] add to these a thousand shops, a hundred places of amusement, . . . brilliantly ornamented churches, and magnificent squares.[1]

By the beginning of the eleventh century, the empire had grown wealthy by controlling trade in the eastern Mediterranean and from the rich farmlands of Asia Minor. It also produced excellent metalwork of all kinds, as well as jewelry, fancy cloth, and other luxury items.

In addition to Constantinople, the Byzantine Empire had several hundred other cities and towns. Two of these cities, Alexandria in Egypt and Antioch in Syria, rivaled the eastern capital in size, wealth, and importance.

At its height, no other power in medieval Europe could rival the Byzantine Empire. According to historian George Ostrogorsky:

> The Byzantine state had at its disposal a unique administrative machine with a . . . well-trained civil service, its military technique was superb, and it possessed an excellent legal system and was based on a highly-developed economic and financial system. It commanded great wealth and . . . in this it differed . . . from other states of . . . the early medieval period.[2]

A Cultural Storehouse

The Byzantine Empire's wealth and power made it important in shaping European history. First, it preserved the ancient Greek and Roman culture on which modern Western civilization is based. Copies of the classical writings of Aristotle, Plato, Sophocles, Virgil, Ovid, and many others, often lost or destroyed in the warfare that preceded and followed the fall of Rome in western Europe, remained safe in Byzantine libraries. As Ostrogorsky remarks, "rooted in the Greek tradition, Byzantium stood for a thousand years as the most important stronghold of culture and learning . . . in the medieval world."[3]

Eventually, Byzantine teachers and scholars would provide much of the intellectual fuel that fed the Renaissance. Additionally, Arabic translations of classical works made their way from the empire into western Europe through Muslim Spain and Sicily.

The Empire and Western Europe

The second important role played by the Byzantine Empire was as a buffer against potential invaders of western Europe. The West was weak and disorganized during the first five centuries following the fall of the western Roman Empire, and thus, its ability to resist strong, determined invaders was very limited. However, the West was spared the full attention of these invaders, who generally chose the Byzantine Empire as their target. The empire, rich in both treasure and culture, was a valuable and tempting prize for would-be conquerors.

Constantinople's access to the Black Sea and the Mediterranean Sea ensured a bustling economy.

This view of Constantinople and the Bosporus shows its well-constructed defenses, which proved impenetrable to attackers lured by the city's wealth and culture.

During the early Middle Ages particularly, the Byzantines repelled Persian and Muslim invasions, and they fought against various nomadic tribes that came out of central Asia. Although some invaders, such as the Bulgars, Avars, and Slavs, did conquer parts of eastern Europe, successful Byzantine resistance kept them from turning their full attention toward western Europe. Throughout the Middle Ages, Constantinople, surrounded by "rushing waters . . . on every side but one, which . . . [was] strongly walled," proved to be one of the world's great fortresses. Its defenses and defenders turned back one group of invaders after another, and "Avars, Persians, Arabs, Bulgarians, and Russians would threaten the . . . capital in turn and fail."[4] Thus, the still struggling and young western kingdoms were not overrun; instead, protected by geography and by determination, they survived and grew, finally evolving into modern Europe.

1 From Rome to Byzantium

The Byzantine Empire had its beginnings in the year 330, when Constantine I, emperor of a Roman empire that stretched from Britain to the Near East, dedicated the city of Constantinople, or as he called it, New Rome. The dedication date, May 11, became an annual holiday.

New Rome

Constantinople was built on the site of the ancient Greek town of Byzantium, and it covered a triangular peninsula bordered on three sides by water. Only the west side, the peninsula's neck, was land, and Constantine had a wall built there to keep out attacking enemies. To the south of the city was the Sea of Marmara, to the east, the Bosporus, and to the north, the Golden Horn—a long, narrow body of water that looks like a horn or a crooked finger. It stretched inland from the Bosporus and was the city's harbor.

Constantinople's construction took only five years. According to historian Will Durant:

> [Constantine] brought in thousands of workmen and artists to raise city walls, fortification, administrative buildings, palaces, and homes; he adorned the squares and streets with fountains . . . and . . . [had] famous sculptures conscripted [taken] . . . from a hundred cities.[5]

The city suffered from this rapid construction, for soon after its dedication, the hastily slapped-together buildings started cracking and crumbling.

After the new city's completion, Constantine moved the imperial capital from Rome to Constantinople. An important reason for this move was political turmoil in Rome. The Italian city was full of battling political parties, many of which traced their history back centuries to the old Roman Republic. Some of these parties wanted a new emperor, while others wanted to limit the emperor's authority or to see the empire ended and the republic restored. The old capital was a dangerous place for the emperor, for civil riot was always possible, and even war.

Division of Empire

Constantinople's population and importance grew rapidly over the next three decades. The old imperial capital, Rome, by

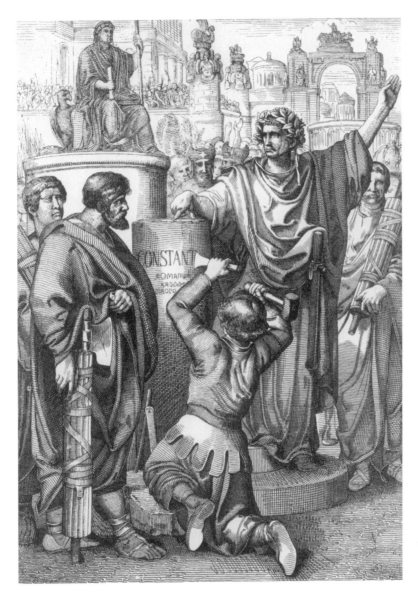

Constantine I, hand raised, renames Byzantium Constantinople in 330. Constantine oversaw the construction of the new city, then moved the capital of the Roman Empire from Rome to Constantinople.

contrast, suffered through hard times. Its population declined, and its public buildings and monuments fell apart from lack of money to repair them. Rome was no longer even an Italian administrative center, Milan having taken over in that capacity.

Even with a new capital, running the empire proved too much for Constantine and his successors. In 364 Emperor Valen-tinian I divided the Roman Empire into western and eastern halves. In place of a single emperor, two co-emperors now ruled, Valentinian in the west and his brother Valens in the east. Constantinople was the capital of the east, Milan, the capital of the west. Later, the naval port of Ravenna on Italy's Adriatic coast became the western capital.

The division was a practical solution to the problems of managing the immense territory of the Roman Empire. The empire at this time covered an area that stretched from the Atlantic Ocean in the west to the Persian Gulf in the east, a distance equal to that between New York City and Los Angeles.

East and West

Valentinian drew the line of division between the Greek-speaking and the Latin-speaking portions of the empire. The east oversaw the Balkan peninsula, Asia Minor, the Near East, and Egypt, while the west controlled Italy, Spain, Gaul (roughly equal to present-day France), Britain, and the western half of North Africa.

The official religion of both parts of the empire was Christianity, with most Christians being members of the Catholic (universal) Church. The emperors were the heads of the church, although in both, East and West, the pope, the bishop of Rome, was eventually recognized by the emperors as the leader of the church.

In theory, the empire was still a single state, but in reality, the halves functioned quite independently of each other. Quarrels and fights between the two were common.

The split was not good for the western half of the Roman Empire because it had a smaller population and less wealth than

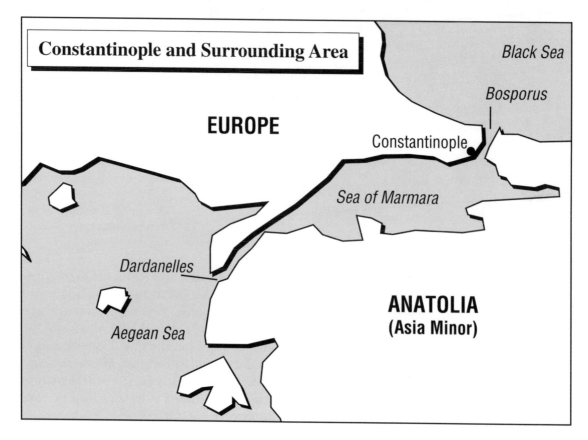

Constantinople and Surrounding Area

Valentinian I divided the Roman Empire into eastern and western halves in 364, each half with its own co-emperor and language: Greek in the East and Latin in the West.

its eastern partner. Also, the western region was not as compact in area as the eastern part and thus not as easily governed. As historian David Nicholas writes, "population density and . . . wealth were much higher in the east than in the west, making it less difficult to support the [imperial government, and] . . . the eastern empire was more easily governable, centered on Asia Minor with a centrally located capital."[6]

Enemies of the Empire

The empire's internal problems were complicated by external threats. In the Near East the aggressive Persian Empire would fight a series of wars with the Romans that would see much bloodshed but little overall change in the balance of power between the two empires.

The second threat to the empire came from fierce Germanic tribes living north of the Danube, which was the empire's northern border in the east. These warlike barbarians constantly raided across the border. Occasionally, Roman armies crossed the Danube and fought pitched battles with the German forces. Until the late fourth century, the empire confined these clashes, as well as large Germanic tribes, to the area north of the Danube.

Germanic Immigrants

The imperial government, however, had no objection to individuals or small family groups entering the empire from Germanic territories. In small numbers, these newcomers posed no threat to the empire's security, and they proved useful, many becoming farm workers and soldiers.

The chief danger was actually to the immigrants, who risked being badly mistreated by imperial officials and citizens. It was not unusual for Germanic people to be sold into slavery or to have their property stolen. Still, they kept coming because they saw the empire as a land of opportunity, and eventually, they were scattered throughout both halves of the empire.

Soldiering was the most popular profession of the Germanic immigrants. By the fourth century, the imperial army was made up of mercenaries, or hired troops, and the warlike people from what is now Germany supplied an endless stream of such mercenaries, serving as both common soldiers and officers. By the beginning of the fifth century, both the eastern and western Roman armies were filled mostly with Germanic mercenaries, a number of whom rose to the rank of general.

The Visigoths, shown here after a victorious battle, sacked the eastern Roman Empire after being abused by imperial officials. This, as well as later Visigoth attacks, alarmed the eastern citizens.

The Visigoths

In 376 some sixty thousand Visigoths, or West Goths, moved south across the Danube and into the eastern Roman Empire, marking the first entrance of a large Germanic tribe into imperial lands. The Goths were not invaders: the eastern emperor had given them permission to settle. However, after eastern officials stole from them, sold their children into slavery, and tried to kill their leader, the Goths became a hostile army that turned against the eastern empire and ravaged the countryside. At Adrianople in 378, a Roman army sent to stop the barbarians' rampage was defeated, and Valens, the eastern emperor, was killed. This defeat and the death of Valens left imperial citizens in both halves of the empire shocked and fearful.

However great the Visigoths' victory at Adrianople, it did not enable them to conquer the eastern empire. Although they attacked Constantinople, they could not take the city. Eventually, after plundering the Balkans, the Goths left the area, turning west, where they struck a deal with the western emperor, who allowed them to settle in imperial territory. In time, the barbarians had a falling out with the western empire, as well, and in 410 they captured and looted Rome, after which they left Italy for Spain.

The news of the plundering of Rome shocked the citizens of the eastern empire even more than the defeat at Adrianople. At Constantinople, the news brought out sixteen thousand volunteers to build a new city wall, which was "13 to 15 feet thick, 30 to 40 feet high, and 4½ miles long, with ninety-six towers."[7] Much of this massive wall still stands today. Later, across the mouth of the Golden Horn, the city stretched a chain that could be raised or lowered to keep out enemy ships. Such measures ensured the city's survival during the many sieges it endured over the next thousand years.

The Fortunes of Empire

After the Visigoths, the imperial defenses began to crumble, and one barbarian army after another made its way into the empire. These various Germanic invaders

---

The Visigoths Enter the Eastern Empire

The Roman historian Ammianus Marcellinus, in his Roman History, *describes the Visigoths' arrival in the eastern Roman Empire. This translation, by C. D. Yonge, was published in 1911.*

"Under the command of their leader Alavivus, [the Visigoths] occupied the banks of the Danube, and sent ambassadors to the emperor Valens, humbly entreating [asking] to be received by him as his subjects. They promised to live quietly, and to furnish a body of . . . troops if necessary. . . .

The affair seemed a cause of joy . . ., according to the skillful flatterers who were always extolling [praising] and exaggerating the good fortune of the emperor. They congratulated him that an embassy [the ambassadors] had come from the farthest corners of the earth, unexpectedly offering him a large body of recruits; and that, by combining the strength of his own people with these foreign forces, he would have an army absolutely invincible [unbeatable]. They observed . . . that the payment for military reinforcements, which came in every year from the provinces, might now be saved and accumulated in his coffers [treasury]. . . .

Full of this hope, [Valens] sent forth several officers to bring this ferocious people and their carts into our territory. . . . [N]o one was left behind, not even of those who were stricken with mortal disease [dying]. . . . [T]he . . . officers who were entrusted with the charge of conducting the . . . barbarians across the river, though they repeatedly endeavored to calculate their numbers, at last abandoned the attempt as hopeless."

grabbed off western territory until little was left of the western empire except Italy. The eastern empire, however, remained intact because it was strong enough to survive such attacks. As historian Crane Brinton observes, "the eastern . . . Empire . . . usually managed to deflect the . . . blows of . . . invaders so that they fell chiefly upon the West. . . . The cities of the East continued prosperous, and government operated undisturbed."[8]

Still, the eastern empire was sometimes badly mauled, as it was when attacked by the non-Germanic barbarians known as the Huns, led by Attila. Theodosius II, the eastern emperor, after losing an army to Attila, finally bought off the Hun leader and his army with large payments of gold.

Yet, despite these invasions, the eastern empire remained stable and prosperous. During the first half of the fifth century,

A Barbarian Victory at Adrianople

In 378, at Adrianople, the Visigoths defeated an eastern Roman army and killed the eastern emperor, Valens. The Roman soldier Ammianus Marcellinus fought at Adrianople and later described the battle in his Roman History.

"Our men came in sight of the wagons of the enemy, which . . . [were] arranged in a circle. According to their custom, the barbarian host [army] raised a fierce and hideous yell, while the Roman generals marshalled [arranged] their line of battle. . . .

And while arms and missiles of all kinds were meeting in fierce conflict, . . . our men began to retreat; but presently . . . they made a fresh stand, and the battle increased . . . terrifying our soldiers, numbers of whom were pierced by strokes of the javelins hurled at them, and by arrows.

Then the two lines of battle dashed against each other. . . . Our left wing had advanced . . . but they were deserted by the rest of the cavalry, and . . . they were . . . beaten down. . . . Presently, our infantry also was left unsupported. . . . The barbarians . . . beat down our horses and men and left no spot to which our ranks could fall back to operate. . . .

Amid all this great . . . confusion our infantry were exhausted by toil and danger, until at last they had neither the strength left to fight nor spirit to plan anything. . . . At last our columns were entirely beaten back. . . .

Scarcely one third of the whole army escaped."

Eastern emperor Theodosius II preferred books to politics, leaving most of the administrative work to his sister, Pulcheria.

these good conditions were due in large part to Pulcheria, the sister of Theodosius II; this competent woman took care of the day-to-day imperial duties and was emperor in all but name. Her brother spent much of his time reading, studying, and illuminating, that is, illustrating manuscripts, the handwritten sets of pages that were bound together into books before the invention of the printing press.

Pulcheria was a smart, hard-nosed politician. Extremely well educated, Pulcheria was only fifteen when she was named her younger brother's regent, a role she retained unofficially even after Theodosius became an adult. Pulcheria, who was also very religious, took her duties so seriously that she vowed never to marry. As the scholar Will Durant observes:

> She . . . dressed with . . . simplicity, fasted, sang hymns, and prayed. . . . The palace was turned into a convent into which only women and a few

priests might enter. Amid all this sanctity [holiness], Pulcheria . . . governed so well that in all forty-two years of Theodosius'. . . reign the Eastern Empire enjoyed exceptional tranquility, while the Western was crumbling into chaos.[9]

One Emperor Again

Indeed, the western empire was crumbling, its armies unable to stop the barbarian invaders. One by one, the western provinces, Britain, Spain, North Africa, and Gaul, were lost to the Germanic tribes, until little was left but Italy.

In 476 a non-Roman, the barbarian Odovacar, overthrew the last western Roman emperor, Romulus Augustulus. Odovacar then struck a bargain with Zeno, the newly crowned eastern emperor. The barbarian would recognize Zeno's authority as sole ruler of the empire. In exchange, Zeno would appoint Odovacar imperial governor of Italy.

Some modern histories label Odovacar's assumption of power as the fall of the Roman Empire. People alive at the time, however, did not think they had experienced the end of an era. Under Odovacar, life in Italy continued much as it had. The scholar Will Durant points out that:

> No one seems to have seen in this event the "fall of Rome"; on the contrary, it seemed to be a blessed unification of the Empire. . . . The Roman Senate saw the matter so, and raised a statue to Zeno. The Germanization of the Italian . . . government . . . seemed

The Huns

The Huns were among the most feared of the many barbarian peoples who threatened the eastern Roman Empire. This description, Ammianus Marcellinus's Roman History, *reflects the prejudices of its Roman author.*

"The . . . Huns . . . are a race [people] savage beyond all parallel. At the very moment of birth the cheeks of their . . . children are marked [branded] by an iron. . . . They . . . are so hardy that they neither require fire nor well-flavored food, but live on . . . roots . . . , or on the half-raw flesh of any animal, which they warm rapidly by placing between their own thighs and the backs of their horses.

They never shelter . . . under roofed houses, but avoid them, as people ordinarily avoid sepulchers [tombs]. . . . [T]hey wander about, roaming over the mountains and the woods and accustom [train] themselves to bear frost and hunger and thirst from their very cradles. . . .

There is not a person in the whole nation who cannot remain on his horse day and night. On horseback they buy and sell, they take their meat and drink, and there they recline on the narrow neck of their steed. . . .

None of them plow [are farmers] . . . , for they have no settled abode, but are homeless and lawless, . . . wandering with their wagons, which they make their homes. . . .

This active . . . race, being excited by an unrestrained desire of plundering the possession of others, went on ravaging and slaughtering all the nations in their neighborhood."

The Huns, depicted here trampling their victims, were a formidable force even for the well-established military of the eastern Empire.

to be negligible [minor] shifts on the surface of the national scene.[10]

The Ostrogoths

Although Odovacar governed Italy well, he was too independent to suit Zeno. The emperor complained that he had lost control of Italy because Odovacar was acting like an independent ruler, not a governor answerable to Zeno. For Zeno, the only way to restore imperial authority in the west was to remove Odovacar.

At the same time, Zeno was facing a problem closer to Constantinople. Settled in the upper Balkans was a Germanic tribe, the Ostrogoths or East Goths. Although the Ostrogoths had pledged their loyalty to the empire, they occasionally raided their imperial neighbors to the south.

Zeno decided that the best way to end these raids was to move the Ostrogoths out of the Balkans. Thus, in 488 he aimed these action-oriented allies toward the south, inviting the Goths to invade Italy and take it from Odovacar. The emperor believed this to be a good plan because it would remove Odovacar and also rid the eastern empire of the Goths. Further, he felt that the leader of the Ostrogoths, Theodoric, who had been raised and educated in Con-

stantinople, would be more controllable than Odovacar. As the historian Norman F. Cantor observes, "Theodoric went to Italy with the understanding that the rights of the emperor in Italy would be preserved. [Zeno] . . . expected that the Ostrogothic invasion would do nothing to decrease imperial sovereignty [authority] there, but would increase its strength."[11]

In 493, under the leadership of Theodoric, the Ostrogoths captured Italy and killed Odovacar. For a time, relations between the emperor and Theodoric were friendly, as the Ostrogoth leader, now known as Theodoric the Great, worked to keep the western empire Roman. The Goth partially succeeding in reforming the imperial government by putting a stop to widespread corruption in the Roman civil service and by lowering taxes. He launched an ambitious program that cleaned up harbors, repaired aqueducts, and restored churches and public buildings.

Within ten years of the Ostrogothic takeover, however, Theodoric, like Odovacar, began operating as though Italy were a separate kingdom, ruled by him. Clearly, Zeno, the Roman emperor, had failed to bring Italy under imperial authority. Still Zeno and his successors ruled over an intact eastern empire, which with the end of the western emperors, had become the Byzantine Empire.

2 Byzantine Society

The Byzantine Empire was a complex and well-organized society, governed by a many-layered bureaucracy. Both the social setup and the government were modeled on Rome. As historian Steven Runciman notes:

> Few states have been organized in a manner so well suited to the times. . . . This organization was not the conscious and deliberate work of a single man or a single moment. . . . [I]t was a heritage from the Roman past, but continually it . . . [was] adapted and supplemented throughout the centuries to suit [the Byzantines'] varying requirements.[12]

The Emperor, Imperial Advisers, and Bureaucrats

As in the Roman Empire, the emperor was at the top of Byzantine government and society. Also known as the *basileus* (Greek for "king"), the Byzantine ruler was the most powerful individual in the empire. His decrees automatically became law, and no one in the empire could overturn these laws.

Those who dealt directly with the emperor conducted themselves according to very strict rules. Imperial etiquette was so complicated that entire books were written on the subject. Historian Crane Brinton observes:

> Silence in . . . [the emperor's] presence was the rule. He spoke and gave his commands through simple, brief, and established formulas. When he gave gifts, his subjects had their hands beneath their cloaks, a . . . gesture implying that the touch of a mere human hand would soil his. . . . On public occasions the emperor was acclaimed [praised] in song, to the sound of silver trumpets.[13]

The emperor was the chief administrator of the empire and was briefed daily on conditions across the Byzantine state by imperial officials and secretaries—men in charge of administrative departments. All government departments operated under the emperor's direct order, because only he had the authority to set policy. It was the emperor who, among other things, determined the amount of tax the average citizen paid, ordered army units from one imperial post to another, and decided how much would be spent on erecting new buildings in Constantinople, the capital.

The Person of the Emperor

In these two excerpts, both found in L. Sprague de Camp's Great Cities of the Ancient World, *John Chrysostom, the patriarch (chief bishop) of Constantinople, first describes the rich dress of the emperor; the Byzantine historian Michael Psellus in his* Chronographia *then explains the problems that arise from the emperor's position in society.*

"The Emperor wears on his head either a diadem [headband], or a crown of gold, decorated with precious stones. . . . These ornaments, and his purple garments are reserved for his sacred person alone; and his robes of silk are embroidered with the figures of gold dragons. His throne is of massy [heavy] gold. Whenever he appears in public, he is surrounded by his courtiers, his guards, and his attendants. . . . The two mules that draw the chariot of the monarch are perfectly white, and shining all over with gold. The [emperor's] chariot . . . [is] pure and solid gold."

"In the case of a private citizen, . . . he is not over-much troubled by outside affairs. . . . How different it is with an emperor, whose private life is never, even in its most intimate detail, allowed respite [rest] from trouble! . . . If he seeks recreation, . . . he incurs [gets] the displeasure of the critics. If he . . . [expresses] kindly sentiments, he is accused of ignorance, and when he arouses himself to show interest, they blame him for being meddlesome [interfering]. If he defends himself or takes . . . reprisals, everyone levels abuse at . . . his 'quick temper.' And as for trying to do anything in secret, [it is impossible]."

The Byzantine emperor held more power than anyone else in the empire. Strict etiquette was required when people interacted with him, reflecting his importance.

In addition to his administrative duties, the emperor was required to preside over all important festivals, holiday games, state banquets, and religious events. As one Byzantine put it, "when there is no [emperor], it is impossible to celebrate the festivals."[14]

The emperor had a number of hand-picked personal advisers who formed a cabinet called the *sacrum consistorium*, the latter word coming from the Latin "to [take a] stand." The *consistorium* met regularly with the emperor to discuss administrative appointments, problems at home and abroad, proposed laws, and daily management of imperial affairs.

The emperor also had the aid of the Byzantine senate, which was modeled on that of Rome. The senate drew up legislation and presented it to the emperor, who might or might not approve. The senate had no power to pass laws of its own.

Below the imperial advisory bodies were many layers of officials and bureaucrats who carried out the emperor's orders. The most important official was the *magister officiorum*, or the master of offices, who appointed the thousands of administrators staffing the various governmental departments. In addition to this duty, the master of offices was in charge of foreign relations, the postal system, and the em-

In this mosaic the emperor is pictured with his many attendants. A large number of people were needed to help the emperor run the empire, including advisers, members of the senate, and various officials and bureaucrats.

Imperial Ceremony

One of the Byzantine emperor's major tasks was taking part in the many festivals, state banquets, and religious events. Bishop Liudprand from Cremona, in northern Italy, quoted in The Eagle, the Crescent, and the Cross: Sources of Medieval History, *edited by Charles T. Davis, describes one such ceremony.*

"In the week before the . . . Feast of Palms [Palm Sunday], the emperor makes a payment in gold coins to his . . . officers of the court, each one receiving a sum proportionate to his office. . . . A table was brought in . . . which had upon it parcels of money tied up in bags, . . . the sum being written on the outside of the bag. The recipients then . . . stood before the king [emperor]. . . . The first to be summoned was the marshal of the palace, who carried off his money, not in his hands but on his shoulders, together with four cloaks of honor [presents indicating the emperor's esteem for the recipient]. After him came the commander in chief of the army and the lord high admiral of the fleet. These being of equal rank received an equal number of money bags and cloaks, which they did not carry off on their shoulders but with some assistance dragged . . . away. . . . Then followed the order of patricians [nobles]. . . . After them came a huge crowd of minor dignitaries . . . [but] this was [not] all done in one day. It began on the fifth day of the week at six . . . in the morning and went on till ten, and the emperor finished his part . . . on the sixth and seventh day."

peror's bodyguard. He was also the empire's spymaster, running a string of twelve hundred informers, whose input allowed him to keep tabs on corrupt and dangerously ambitious officials.

Imperial Succession

The emperorship was not hereditary, although emperors appointed their own heirs. Most emperors chose a son as successor, but others selected a close and trusted friend or adviser. Even when the Byzantine ruler picked a family member as the imperial heir, he did not necessarily choose the eldest son, or even a son at all, but rather the relative who seemed best suited for the job. If the heir were not the emperor's son, the Byzantine ruler normally adopted him so that the emperorship would remain in the family and the dynasty would continue.

Emperors tended to select their successors either late in life or when they knew they were dying. When a successor was named, he was made co-ruler with the reigning emperor so that he could begin learning the imperial duties.

Checks and Balances

The emperor may have had more power than any other person in the Byzantine Empire, but he was not all-powerful. Although he chose his own successor, that heir could not be crowned until he had been formally elected by members of three groups, whose votes were counted separately: the senate, the army, and the citizens of the empire.

Emperors could also be removed from office. An incompetent or disliked emperor could be voted out by one of the three sets of electors, or he could be overthrown by armed revolt. Revolts against the imperial ruler were common, and over the centuries, emperors were killed, imprisoned, and exiled. Many were also blinded, an act that made them unacceptable to hold the throne. As author Harold Lamb points out, this powerful ruler had to be constantly on his guard:

> He was . . . emperor of the Romans. He was master of Byzantium, . . . tyrant [absolute ruler], . . . general-in-chief. . . . He could slay any man with a whispered word or build a walled city with the scrawl of a pen dipped in red ink; but he himself must watch without seeming to do so for the gleam of an assassin's dagger, or listen . . . for the murmur of the . . . mob that meant revolt.[15]

Despite the several dozen emperors overthrown during the empire's thousand-

Empresses could play an active role in Byzantine politics along with emperors, but they did not participate in public events, usually remaining in the palace.

year history, the need for a supreme leader was never questioned. An overthrown ruler was replaced by either another emperor or by two co-emperors.

Empresses

Except for the brief period when an imperial heir was co-ruler, there was only one emperor at a time. However, there could be any number of empresses. Besides the emperor's wife, other women related to the ruler could also be empresses. In the fifth century, for example, Pulcheria, the sister of Emperor Theodosius II, was empress along with her brother's wife.

Except for church services, empresses were rarely seen outside the royal palace. Unlike the emperor, they did not take part in public parades or festivals. Some even spent their lives in special women's quarters in the palace.

However, empresses were not barred from helping the emperor run the government, and a number sat in on councils or took care of day-to-day imperial duties. If the emperor died without naming an heir, that duty fell to the empress. As a rule, the empress often gave up her active role in government upon the election of her chosen successor.

An empress could even become the head of the Byzantine Empire, usually as a regent, that is, administrator for an underage monarch. On rare occasions, however, the empress was sole ruler, as with the Empress Irene in the eighth century.

The Army

Supporting the efforts of the emperor and the Byzantine administration was the military. As the scholar Steven Runciman observes, "the administration of Byzantium was closely bound up with her military forces. The empire was beset with [constantly harassed by] enemies; never for a moment could the Government feel free from the danger of foreign invasion."[16]

The Byzantine army was the most important part of the Byzantine military. It depended on achieving success in battle by carefully training and equipping its troops. The infantry was supplied with well-made steel swords, spears, and armor, and the cavalry with strong lances and bows.

At the head of the 120,000-soldier army was the emperor, and in fact many emperors actually led their troops into battle. Below the emperor were six generals in chief, each of whom was in charge of one of the empire's military districts.

Stationed in these districts were several regiments, each having between three and four thousand soldiers. There were both infantry and cavalry regiments, each commanded by a general. Junior officers and noncommissioned officers led smaller units within each regiment, such units varying in size and number. Supporting the regiments were signal corps that used mirrors to flash messages back and forth, medical corps, and intelligence corps.

Empress Irene was an exception to the usual female rulers; instead of co-ruling with an emperor or acting as a regent, she headed the empire herself.

This Byzantine soldier (left) is equipped with strong armor, a shield, and a sword. To fend off the numerous enemy attacks, the army was highly trained and well supplied.

The army's role in Byzantine society was not confined to defense. It was also more important than the senate and the citizens at large when it came to selecting the emperor. Knowing the power of the army, some emperors made sure that it was solidly behind the imperial heir. In the eighth century, for instance, Emperor Leo IV wished to be succeeded by his young son. Therefore he secured the written approval of his choice from the entire army, including units stationed at the imperial borders.

The Navy

The Byzantine navy was much smaller than the army, with only a single admiral in chief reporting to the emperor. The naval forces commanded by this officer were divided into fleets of warships, each vessel carrying one hundred to three hundred sailors.

The Byzantine navy had one of the first secret weapons in warfare, Greek fire. Although its exact nature is now unknown, Greek fire probably contained petroleum. It was pumped into bronze lion heads mounted on warships and then shot across the water to set enemy vessels on fire. Greek fire was a fearsome weapon in the Middle Ages because it ignited when exposed to air; worse yet, the flames could not be put out with water; a property supporting the theory that the material was a petroleum product.

Byzantine Diplomacy

Despite its well-armed army and navy, the Byzantine Empire preferred negotiation to war. Byzantine diplomatic missions were often very successful, and their records show shrewd thinking and planning, accompanied by sharp bargaining.

Imperial agents kept track of affairs in all nearby states not under Byzantine control. Through these agents, the imperial government provided money to pro-Byzantine factions, encouraging them to rebel against any rulers who threatened war with the empire.

The Byzantine emperors saw to it that whenever possible, the sons of foreign leaders were educated in Constantinople. When the guest students returned to their homes, they brought with them a taste for Byzantine civilization. Peace with the empire was the only way for these men, who soon would be leaders in their own right, to have continued access to Byzantine luxuries and learning.

The emperors also arranged marriages between women of the Byzantine nobility and important local rulers. Sometimes, an emperor married a non-Byzantine princess if he thought the arrangement would be the best way to create a bond with another state.

The Byzantine Economy

The Byzantine Empire was an expensive operation, its bureaucracy and its many wars and diplomatic efforts costly. Yet, despite the occasional economic crisis, the empire's finances were sound because, as the major trade center between Europe and Asia, it was rich. As historian Will Durant writes, "from the fifth century to the fifteenth Constantinople remained the greatest market and shipping center in the world," for "Roman roads and bridges were kept in repair, and . . . fleets . . . bound the capital with a hundred ports in East and West."[17] The imperial economy was so strong that the *nomisma*, the Byzantine gold piece, was the standard coin throughout the entire Mediterranean region for over eight hundred years.

Merchant ships conduct their business in Constantinople. The empire's great expenses were supported by the capital's vibrant economy; it was the heart of trade in both Europe and Asia.

At the heart of the Byzantine economy were very successful state-controlled businesses and industries, such as farms, cattle ranches, marble quarries, and gold and silver mines. Also, the empire's treasury was helped by imperial monopolies of silk, purple dye, and gold embroidery, all important trade goods that were used for the ceremonial clothing of civil and religious leaders all over Europe, the Near East, and North Africa. The rest of the empire's income came from taxes on everything from sales to property to inheritance.

The Aristocracy

As in many other societies, the Byzantine Empire's riches were in the hands of a wealthy few, who enjoyed all possible luxuries and privileges. Yet whereas in most of

---

An Outsider Views the Emperor

Outsiders visiting the Byzantine Empire were generally impressed by much of what they saw, particularly since the Byzantines had more advanced technical skills than most of their guests. Here, as quoted in The Eagle, the Crescent, and the Cross, *Bishop Liudprand of Cremona describes a visit to the imperial court.*

"Before the emperor's seat stood a tree, made of bronze gilded over [covered with gold], whose branches were filled with birds, also made of gilded bronze, which uttered [gave out] different cries, each according to its varying species. The throne itself was . . . of immense size and was guarded by lions, made either of bronze or of wood covered over with gold, who beat the ground with their tails and gave a dreadful roar with open mouth and quivering tongue . . . [A]fter I had three times made obeisance [shown respect] to the emperor with my face upon the ground, I lifted my head . . . [and the emperor,] whom just before I had seen sitting on a moderately elevated seat had now changed his raiment [clothes] and was sitting on the level of the ceiling. . . .

The emperor . . . invited me to dinner with him. . . . The emperor and his guests . . . recline on couches: and everything is served in vessels, not of silver, but of gold. . . . [T]he solid food fruit is brought on in . . . golden bowls, which are too heavy for men to lift. . . . Through openings in the ceiling hang three ropes . . . with golden rings. These rings are attached to the handles . . . [of] the bowls, and with four or five men helping from below, they [the bowls] are swung on to the table."

Europe, mastering the trade of war was the route to nobility, in the empire, it was money. Although many in the aristocracy were of Roman descent, anyone with the money could buy a title, which is what wealthy merchants and landowners often did. High church officials were also a part of the nobility.

Most of the noblemen held government positions, which took up a portion of their time. The rest was spent with their wives, either attending functions at the imperial court or presiding over their own, smaller courts.

Many members of the aristocracy had both town and country homes but preferred living in the city, visiting their country estates only in the summer. The two-story houses of the rich were built like those of Rome. Each house faced inward to an open courtyard, its exterior walls blank, except for the owner's name carved on the wall facing the street. The inner courtyard, which contained the well from which the household got its water, was generally large enough for the owner to exercise his horses, whose stable opened onto the court.

Carved wooden or stone columns supported the second story, which was reached by stairway, wooden in most houses but marble in the residences of the wealthiest. The only windows looked out onto the inner courtyard. Beginning in the fifth century, in Constantinople, some taller houses appeared, with a line of upper floor windows looking out over the street.

The Middle Class

The Byzantine Empire had a very small middle class, which was mostly found in

An elaborately dressed and armed eunuch guards the bath. Since eunuchs could not become emperor, their status prevented them from seizing the throne.

the cities. Small-scale merchants and shop owners were among those who belonged to this class. They lived less well than the nobility, but most could afford at least one or two servants.

Ambitious members of the middle class made their way into the aristocracy. Sometimes, their entry was through a successful business, other times, education, the army, or marriage.

Many of the highest offices in the Byzantine civil service could be held only by eunuchs, that is, men who had been castrated. In addition, it was common for the heads of the army and the navy to be eunuchs. There was a law, as well, stating that a eunuch could not be emperor. Thus it was pointless for high imperial officials, who might have been tempted to try to seize the throne, to plot against the legal ruler. A bizarre side effect of this law was that aristocratic and middle-class families routinely castrated one or more of their own sons. Such castration put these sons on the fast track to government promotion.

The City Poor

The largest group of people in the empire was the working class, and those belonging to this class were mostly poor. The poor did not starve in the cities, however: the labor for public works projects, such as repairing aqueducts and maintaining parks, was supplied by men who worked for food. Also, the emperor provided orphanages, poorhouses (homeless shelters), and hospitals for the poor.

The urban poor were mostly laborers, who lived in squalor. A few had small shanties, "roofed with rushes and with beaten earth floors."[18] Most lived in wooden tenements that were five to nine stories high. Unlike most twentieth-century cities, where rich and poor generally live in separate neighborhoods, the housing of the Byzantine poor surrounded the palaces of the rich. Indeed, the worst slum in Constantinople ringed the emperor's Great Palace.

The Country Poor

In the country, peasants, living in simple huts and working small plots of land, composed the working poor. On the whole, the peasants were much worse off than city laborers. The country poor were drained by a combination of taxes and rents to landlords. The imperial government had "lifted the tax from trade and industry and imposed it . . . on the peasants. . . . Throughout the whole of Byzantium's history the taxes imposed upon the agricultural community were such as to undermine their well-being."[19]

These peasants could not even escape their land. Some were chained to it because they were serfs, whose positions of dependence were passed by inheritance from parent to child. Serfs could not leave a farm without the landlord's permission, for this was one of the conditions of their bondage.

Others were tenant farmers, who although technically free, were as fixed in place as the serfs. The government made it difficult for free peasants to leave their farms because to feed the large urban populations, the Byzantine state needed people to work every acre of farmland. To leave the land, a free farmer had to pay off all taxes that both he and his children were liable for in their lifetimes. Additionally, an ambitious peasant's neighbors were motivated to prevent his leaving by the existence of a second tax, one paid by each farming community as a whole. If any farmer left, the others in his community had to continue paying his share of the tax.

In both city and country, there were also large numbers of slaves; some were privately owned, and some belonged to the state. Government slaves worked in mines and on state farms, while privately owned slaves were household servants. The former led brutal, often short lives,

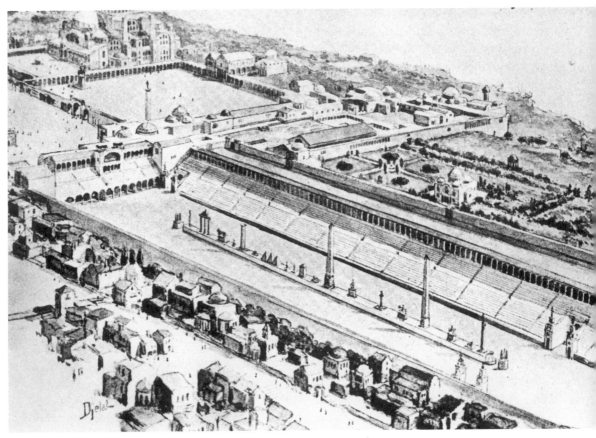

The Constantinople Hippodrome hosted sporting and theater events and religious ceremonies, but mainly chariot races, which were popular in all levels of society.

while the latter generally lived comfortably. Only non-Christians were enslaved, since the Byzantines interpreted their religion as forbidding Christians from keeping fellow Christians as slaves.

The Hippodromes

Unlike the peasants, the city poor had one avenue of escape: the free entertainment at the hippodromes. The hippodromes, which were attended also by the middle class and the aristocracy, were stadiums designed primarily for chariot racing. However, they also hosted athletic contests, plays, comedy acts, and wild animal shows. They were used for important religious ceremonies, political rallies, the displaying of war captives and loot, and even the public torturing of important prisoners.

But chariot racing was the centerpiece of the hippodromes, for as in the Roman Empire, chariot racing was extremely popular, even more than football, baseball, or basketball is in the present-day United States. The closest parallel in the modern world to the Byzantine chariot-racing phenomenon can be seen in the enthusiasm aroused by the national soccer teams in some countries.

Chariot racing was at its most dramatic at the forty-thousand-seat Constantinople Hippodrome. Along a circular course over a half mile in length, ten chariots thundered, sometimes four abreast, for seven laps. Each day of racing saw eight competitions. Although set at an earlier date, the 1959 movie *Ben-Hur* conveys an excellent sense of the danger and excitement of these races.

The charioteers, or drivers, were admired as heroes, particularly among the working class, which provided most of the racers. But they were more than sim-

ply sports heroes. They and their teams, and the colors worn by those teams, became associated with the two major Byzantine political parties, the Blues and the Greens.

Politics in Byzantium: The Blues versus the Greens

The Blues and the Greens gave imperial citizens a way of venting their political frustrations. One faction would normally back the government, while the other opposed it. Occasionally, the two parties joined together in common cause against the emperor. Tax hikes and unpopular wars often led to these Blue-Green alliances. Members

One charioteer edges in front of another as they prepare to round the corner.

The Blues and the Greens

The Blues and the Greens were Byzantine chariot racing teams, whose followers formed into political parties. In these two excerpts, the first taken from the History of the Wars, *as quoted in* Great Cities of the Ancient World, *and the second from the* Secret History, *the Byzantine historian Procopius describes first the mentality of the Blues and the Greens and second how some of the Blues took to setting themselves apart from the rest of the Byzantines.*

"There grows up in them against their fellow men a hostility which has no cause, and at no time does it cease or disappear, for it gives place neither to the ties of marriage nor of relationship, and the case is the same even though those who differ in any respect to these colors be brothers or any other kin [relatives]. They care neither for things divine nor human in these struggles."

"[The Blues] revolutionized the style of wearing their hair. . . . [T]hey allowed [it] to keep on growing as long as it would . . . but [decided on] clipping the hair short on the front of the head down to the temples, and letting it hang down in great length and disorder in the back. . . . This weird combination they called the Hun haircut. . . .

[T]he sleeves of their tunics [shirts] were cut tight about the wrists, while from there to the shoulders they were of . . . [a large] fullness; . . . whenever they moved their hands, as when applauding at the theater or encouraging a driver in the Hippodrome, these immense sleeves fluttered conspicuously. . . . Their cloaks, trousers, and boots were also different: . . . these too were called the Hun style."

of the two parties also enlisted in the city watch or militia and helped to keep the city walls in repair.

Large numbers of the working poor belonged to both the Blues and the Greens. However, the leadership of both parties tended to come from other segments of Byzantine society. The Blues leaders came from the aristocracy, while the Greens were drawn from the merchant class.

As important as chariot racing and its political associations were to the Byzantines, both paled in comparison to religion. Byzantine Christianity colored every aspect of the society and every action of the government. It was the axis on which the whole society turned.

3 Byzantine Christianity

The Christian church was central to the culture of the Byzantine Empire. Religion went very deep in the empire's society, ruling every part of Byzantine life. As historian Crane Brinton observes:

> At every important moment in the life of every person, the Church played an important role, governing marriage, and family relations, filling leisure time, helping to determine any critical decision. . . . [T]he most serious intellectual problems . . . were those of theology, and they were attacked with zest [gusto] by brains second to none in power. . . . [T]he arts were largely . . . devoted to the representation of ecclesiastical [religious] subjects. . . . [B]usiness was carried on under the auspices [authoritative guidance] of the Church.[20]

All Byzantine citizens, from laborers to merchants to aristocrats, took part in religious debates about such subjects as how exactly God, Christ, and the Holy Spirit were related to each other and whether Satan or God was more powerful on earth. They argued religion during work breaks, in shops, at mealtimes, in taverns, or in any other place where Byzantines stopped to talk. For example, if two neighbors met on the street, within minutes, they would

A church built during the Byzantine Empire remains long after the empire's collapse. The Christian church played a vital role in Byzantine life.

be talking about religion. One might fiercely claim that a priest who had sinned could no longer perform his holy duties, while the other, just as forcefully, would argue that he could.

Beliefs

The central belief of Byzantine Christianity, as with all forms of Christianity, was the acceptance of Jesus of Nazareth as Christ, the Savior. The eastern church also recognized the Trinity, composed of God the father, Christ, and the Holy Spirit.

In addition to a belief in salvation and the Trinity, good church members felt that self-discipline, moderation, self-denial, and charity were virtues. Unlike western European Christians, who saw this world as a testing ground leading to a better time in the afterlife, Byzantine Christians were "eager to enter into a state of grace, the right relationship to God, here and now."[21] Nor did the eastern church spend much time speculating on the nature of the afterlife.

In the West, much was written on how to achieve salvation. In the East, such instruction was less common. Eastern

Christianity by Imperial Order

These excerpts, quoted from Creeds, Councils, and Controversies *by J. Stevenson, are from decrees against, first, pagans and then, heretics, as given by Emperor Theodosius I.*

"No person shall pollute himself with sacrificial animals; no person shall slaughter an innocent victim; no person shall approach the [pagan] shrines, shall wander through the temples, or revere [worship] the images formed by mortal labor, lest he become guilty by divine and human laws [of idol worship]. Judges shall also be bound by the general rule that if any man should be devoted to profane [unholy] rites and should enter a [pagan] temple for the purpose of worship . . ., he shall immediately be compelled to pay fifteen pounds of gold."

"We [Theodosius I] decree that whosoever has remained in heretical errors, and either ordains [appoints] clergy, or undertakes clerical office should be fined ten pounds of gold each, and the land . . . on which the forbidden acts are being attempted should, if the connivance [cooperation] of the owner is evident, be added to the resources of our treasury.

We particularly wish to guard against a tenant or a steward [caretaker] of a villa [house] on imperial or public land giving permission for [heretical] assembly; if found guilty, he will be fined ten pounds of gold and this should be . . . collected from each [offender]."

Christians thought that each person could find his or her own way to salvation, as long as that way was approved by the church.

Church Structure

The basic hierarchy of the Byzantine church, that is, its form of government, was established early. At the bottom of the church's clergy were the priests, then came the bishops, and finally, at the top, the emperor.

This early-thirteenth-century Byzantine illustration depicts Jesus in the center. Both the Western and Eastern Churches recognized Jesus as the Savior.

Priests made up the largest part of the clergy, with each priest associated with a single church. Priests sometimes received formal training before being appointed by higher church officials to specific locations.

The running of the Byzantine church fell mostly to the bishops. Each bishop was believed to be a direct spiritual heir of Christ, and each was in charge of a large area known as a bishopric or a see that contained several churches. Sometimes, an archbishop was placed over several bishoprics. The bishops formed religious councils that decided which Christian writings were divinely inspired, who were the true prophets, and which religious practices should be accepted.

The Emperor and the Patriarch of Constantinople

No separation existed between church and state during the Byzantine Empire; the emperor headed both. He was the ambassador of God on earth, and when he rode out to war, he went as God's champion and the defender of Christianity.

The emperor seldom concerned himself with the day-to-day running of the eastern church, confining his activities in this sphere to those required by custom and law. He left church administration to the highest ranking Byzantine bishop, the patriarch of Constantinople.

This highest bishop of the eastern church was elected by the church's other bishops, from among candidates nominated by the emperor. A patriarch who displeased the Byzantine ruler would soon find himself deposed and in exile. An angry emperor need only call a church

A Byzantine bishop, center, was believed to be a direct spiritual heir of Christ. Bishops discerned which writings were divinely inspired and who the true prophets were.

The earliest form of monasticism was practiced by a few hundred individuals living as hermits in deserts, swamps, and mountains. To these holy hermits, the church had become too concerned with worldly wealth and power and had thus suffered a loss of spiritual values. The scholar David Nicholas writes:

> As the Church prospered . . ., many thoughtful Christians were disturbed by the changes [it] had undergone . . ., particularly its growing wealth. Far from attempting to escape the snares of the world, church leaders sought to strengthen their position . . . by accumulating wealth. . . . [A] growing number of persons . . . sought to escape the material world by living in isolation as hermits.[23]

In addition to prayer, these hermits, or anchorites as they were called, put themselves through all sorts of physical trials. Some went without sleep for a week or more, others ate only once a week, and still others carried heavy weights day and night. Self-inflicted wounds and whippings were also practiced. A few devout believers, known as stylites, climbed to the top of sixty-foot-high columns and remained standing there for the rest of their lives.

The anchorites and stylites soon gave way to a second type of monasticism, the monastic orders, which maintained monasteries for men and convents for women. The rules of monastic orders required that the monks and nuns follow strict rules, normally the giving up of all possessions, including property, money, and personal clothing. Monks and nuns spent much of their time at religious worship and study and the rest working in the order's fields, to make the monastery or

council, whose members he had handpicked, to have a troublesome patriarch removed from office. Thus, the emperor could truly say that in addition to "the Grace of God," "this man is appointed Patriarch of Constantinople . . . by [my] Imperial Authority."[22]

Holy Hermits, Monasteries, and Monks

In addition to the priests and bishops, the church recognized as holy men and women who were part of the monastic movement. In monasticism, people withdraw from society to devote most of their time to prayer and meditation.

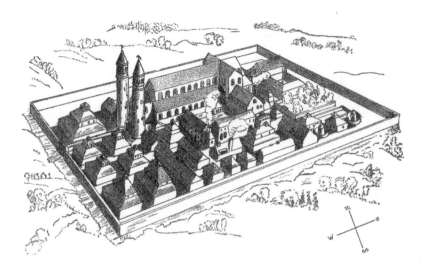

This walled-in monastery shows the seclusion of religious communities in Byzantium. Monks and nuns, who lived in convents, strove for self-sufficiency to have less contact with the outside world and to focus on prayer and contemplation.

convent as self-sufficient as possible. Many residents of monasteries and convents had virtually no contact with the outside world, although others, particularly monastery leaders, were extremely active in church and civil politics.

Monks were part of the clergy, many serving as chaplains to the largest Byzantine churches, which were often attached to monasteries. Monks also had a special place in Byzantine society because the quiet meditation of the monastery appealed to many in the Byzantine Empire. As Steven Runciman observes, "though the splendor of their life was designed as a homage [honor] to God, the Byzantines most admired those who gave up the pleasures of the world and prepared themselves for eternity by contemplation."[24]

Rome and the Pope

The church that the Byzantine emperor and the patriarch of Constantinople oversaw was as Christian as that found in western Europe, and until the eleventh century, the two churches were a single organization. From the beginning, however, rivalry and jealousy existed between the two branches.

The most important bishop in the western church was the pope, the bishop of Rome. The pope's authority came in large part from his location, since even long after the western Roman Empire collapsed, Rome was seen by West and East as a center of power. Rome was the city from which most civil court decisions had come, so it was logical for the bishop of Rome to settle the tricky issues of Christianity.

The pope's authority was also based on a legend that the first bishop of Rome had been St. Peter, seen by many Christians as Jesus' most important disciple. Further, the ruling of an early church council gave Rome authority over Constantinople because the Italian city was the older of the two.

Friction arose between the eastern and western branches of the church because the pope refused to acknowledge the emperor as head of the church. As far as Rome was concerned, no civil leader could outrank the church's spiritual leader. The pope also refused to recognize the patriarch of Constantinople as the second highest official in the church, despite a ruling by a church council to that effect.

Doctrine and Heresy

Rome, however, was not the only important Christian center with which Constantinople had uneasy relations. Both Alexandria in Egypt and Antioch in Syria had patriarchs who ranked just after that of Constantinople. A good deal of political rivalry existed between the three Byzantine cities because they were about equal in size and wealth. However, all the political power resided in Constantinople. These political jealousies spilled over into church affairs, with all three patriarchs jockeying for power within the church.

Much of this power struggle revolved around determining church doctrine or teachings. It was not always clear what beliefs and teachings the church should support. Many interpretations existed with respect to what Jesus had taught and even what he was. For example, the fourth-century priest Arius of Alexandria proposed that God was superior to Christ because God had fathered Jesus. The opposing view was that God and Christ, along with the Holy Spirit, were equal parts of the single being known as the Trinity.

The church generally dealt with opposing doctrines by calling a church council. The attending bishops would listen to all the arguments and then decide which position to support. In two such councils, in 325 and 381, the church sided with the opponents of Arius. Beliefs, that are formally rejected by the church, as in the case of Arius, are called heresies.

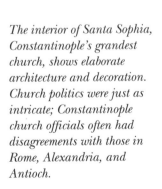

The interior of Santa Sophia, Constantinople's grandest church, shows elaborate architecture and decoration. Church politics were just as intricate; Constantinople church officials often had disagreements with those in Rome, Alexandria, and Antioch.

Life in a Monastery

In this account excerpted in Creeds, Councils, and Controversies, *St. Jerome, who died in about 420, describes life in an early Christian monastery.*

"[The monks] live . . . in separate cells. . . . No monk may visit another before the ninth hour, except the leaders . . ., whose office [task] is to comfort with soothing words, those whose thoughts disquiet [upset] them. After the ninth hour they meet together to sing psalms and read the Scriptures. . . . [W]hen the prayers have ended . . ., one called the father . . . begins to expound [lecture]. . . . After this meeting breaks up . . . [they eat]. . . . [N]o one talks while eating. Bread . . . [and] greens form their fare [food], and the only seasoning is salt and oil. . . .

When the meal is over they . . . return to their dwellings. There each one talks till evening with his comrade thus: 'Have you noticed so-and-so. What grace he has! How silent he is! How soberly he walks!' . . . at night, besides the public prayers, each man keeps vigil [watch] in his own chamber, they [the leaders] go round all the cells . . . [and] carefully ascertain [determine] what their occupants are doing. If they find a monk slothful [lazy], they do not scold him; . . . but they visit him more frequently. . . . Every Lord's day [Sunday] they spend their whole time in prayer and reading; indeed, . . . these are their usual occupations at all times. Every day they learn by heart a portion of the Scripture."

Monasteries, like this one, were somber places whose occupants devoted themselves to prayer and study.

Monophysitism

In the fifth century over a heresy called Monophysitism, Constantinople found itself in a struggle with Alexandria. Monophysitism dealt with the nature of Christ. Christian thought ran that since Jesus had been born a man, he was human, but since he was also a part of the Trinity, he was also divine.

The Monophysites had concluded that Christ's nature was completely divine. They argued that the part of Christ that was human no longer existed because it had been swallowed up and absorbed by the divine. Thus, nothing but Christ's divine nature remained. Their opponents, on the other hand, believed that Christ's nature was an equal mixture of divine and human.

Alexandria was the center of Monophysitism, while Constantinople held to the opposing view of Christ's nature, as did Rome. Pope Leo I sided with Flavian, the patriarch of Constantinople, because as the historian Aikaterina Christophilopoulou writes, "the Roman Church looked with an unfavorable eye on the growing power and ambitious designs of the patriarchal throne of Alexandria, and found it a convenient opportunity to assist in the humiliation of a troublesome rival."[25] However, humiliating Dioscurus, the patriarch of Alexandria, proved difficult.

To decide the Monophysitism issue, Leo called a church council at Ephesus, in western Asia Minor, in 449. At the council, the patriarch Dioscurus arrived with a large party of Alexandrian clergy. Among Dioscurus's followers was a group of thuggish priests who physically threatened and intimidated the other attendees into approving Monophysitism.

The Alexandrians' tactics led to a storm of protest and a labeling of the meeting as the Robber Council. As a result, the Ephesus council's decision was not accepted, and a new council was held in 451 at Chalcedon, across the Bosporus from Constantinople. At Rome and Constantinople's urging, the Council of Chalcedon accepted the view that Christ was an equal mixture of God and human: "Christ was pronounced to have two natures, without confusion . . . but without division or separation, each nature . . . concurring [harmonizing] into one person."[26]

Heretics and Pagans

The Council of Chalcedon also removed Dioscurus from the office of patriarch and declared Monophysitism a heresy. When the church ruled a doctrine heretical, it did its best to stamp out that belief. Religious fanatics would sometimes seek out and harass or kill heretics, but the major weapon against heresy in the Byzantine church was civil law, with the emperor decreeing punishment for convicted heretics. Initially, under the fourth-century emperor Theodosius I, heretics faced heavy fines and loss of their property. Later emperors would pass harsher laws that relied on torture and even execution to eliminate heresy.

Similar laws were also aimed at destroying any pagan or non-Christian religion practiced in the empire. The major target for these laws was the old Greek and Roman religion. Pagans were forbidden to worship, and they were fined if caught doing so. Their temples were torn down or converted to other uses. Known pagans, if

One of the mosaics found in Santa Sophia. The Byzantines' zeal for Christianity led them to persecute those who did not share their beliefs, including pagans, heretics, and Jews.

they ventured out in public, might be attacked and killed by anti-pagan mobs.

Restrictions were also placed on Jews, who could worship only if they paid taxes so high that many had to choose between giving up an important part of their religion and selling their children into slavery. Imperial law demanded the death penalty for any Jew who married a Christian. Like heretics and pagans, Jews were the target of rampaging mobs, who killed any Jew they found and burned down synagogues.

Religion and Revolt

Heavy persecution destroyed the old classical pagan religion, which had been dying even before Christianity became the state religion of Rome in 313. However, persecution was not effective against the Jews or against Christian heretics, who clung doggedly to their beliefs.

Some heresies even flourished under the empire's oppressive laws. Mono-physitism was one of them. Even after the Council of Chalcedon, the citizens of Alexandria refused to give up their belief, which became a symbol of resistance to the central imperial authority. Antioch, the other great rival of Constantinople, also embraced Monophysitism. As historian George Ostrogorsky writes:

> The conflict between the . . . Church of Constantinople and the . . . Churches of the Christian East became the burning problem in ecclesiastical [religious] and secular [civil] politics of the early Byzantine Empire. Monophysitism served as an outlet for the political separatist tendencies of Egypt and Syria; it was the rallying cry of . . . opposition to Byzantine rule.[27]

Religious persecution was the darker side of Byzantine Christianity. On a more positive note, Christianity fused with the old classical culture to create the unique art and writings of the Byzantine Empire.

4 Byzantine Culture

During most of the Middle Ages, the Byzantine Empire's culture was unrivaled in Europe. The empire's wealth gained from trade helped support an excellent school system and a dynamic arts scene.

The core of this culture was Constantinople, with its many teachers, artists, writers, and theologians. Although Alexandria and Antioch were also important cultural centers, it was in the imperial capital that the empire's Greek and Roman past merged most fully with Christian and Near Eastern influences to produce the Byzantine culture.

The Byzantines, like any people, borrowed from others, particularly from their Greek and Roman past. Whereas much classical Greek and Latin writing was lost in the West, most was saved in the Byzantine Empire's libraries and served to guide Byzantine thinking, writing, and teaching.

This classical treasure chest of the Byzantine Empire would be extremely important to western Europe. In the thirteenth and fourteenth centuries, the writings of the Greek philosopher Aristotle would be a major influence that shaped western European culture, and all the surviving ancient Greek and Roman writers would be crucial in creating the culture of Renaissance Europe and, consequently, that of the modern world. As historian Crane Brinton points out, "had it not been for Byzantium, it seems certain that Plato and Aristotle, Homer and Sophocles would have been lost. We cannot even imagine what such a loss would have meant to western civilization." [28]

Near Eastern and Christian Influences

In addition to these classical roots, Byzantine culture was affected by the empire's relationships with Near Eastern societies, particularly the Persian Empire. For example, from Persia, the Byzantines borrowed the complex of rituals surrounding the emperor. They also replaced undecorated Roman togas with Persian silk coats sporting fancy designs. As the scholar Will Durant notes, "from . . . Persia, from . . . Syria, from . . . Egypt, Eastern . . . influences poured into Byzantium. . . . The East preferred . . . rich ornament to stern simplicity, gorgeous silks to shapeless togas." [29]

As with other parts of Byzantine society, the culture reflected the deep Christianity of the people. The church tried at times to eliminate the Greek and Roman features of the culture, for, with rare exceptions, the clergy did not approve of

Ancient Greek philosopher Aristotle instructs a student. Aristotle's writings, along with those of other important Greek and Roman figures, were preserved in Byzantine libraries, shaping Byzantine culture and later Western culture.

the classical works, which they viewed as anti-Christian. Despite it's increasing role in Byzantine education, however, the church failed completely to stamp out pre-Christian learning.

Learning in the Byzantine Empire

The foundation on which Byzantine culture rested was education. The Byzantines had inherited from their Greek and Roman ancestors a deep love and respect for learning. Every Byzantine desired a good education, and the lack of one was considered a serious handicap.

Learning was pursued in a large variety of schools, including the imperial university at Constantinople. As historian David Nicholas notes, "primary education was available even in some smaller villages for both sexes: although formal higher ed-

ucation was normally restricted to men, many aristocratic women studied under tutors."[30] Tutoring was also common for middle- and upper-class children, but state-run schools were available to the children of any free citizen.

A child's education generally began at home, where he or she learned the basics of writing and proper speech. Upon entering school, children received further training in these and other subjects. As the scholar Tamara Talbot Rice writes:

Children were first instructed in grammar—a term which included reading and writing. This was followed by more advanced grammar . . . and introduction to the classics; each pupil was expected to learn 50 lines of Homer by heart each day. . . . At the age of 14 . . . their time was spent in studying rhetoric [the effective use of language in speech and writing]: this included pronunciation and . . . the study of great prose writers. . . . [They] were taught philosophy, the sciences, and the "four arts"—arithmetic, geometry, music, and astronomy.[31]

All these subjects were deeply rooted in the empire's classical heritage. But, in all cases, the subjects were presented in the light of the accepted teachings of the church. To keep the education Christian, pagan schools, such as the Platonic Academy in Athens, were shut down in the sixth century.

Just what proportion of the Byzantines received public or private schooling is unknown, although it was nowhere near 100 percent. Even the exact percentage of the Byzantine population that could read and write is not known. However, most upper and middle-class men and women were literate, as were some of the working class.

Byzantine Teachers

Byzantine teachers were important members of society. Except for private tutors, teachers, including university professors, were paid by either the imperial or the local government. They also had to pass state examinations and possess a license to teach.

One of the most famous Byzantine professors was the fifth-century philosopher and mathematician Hypatia, who was a follower of the Greek philosopher Plato and a lifelong resident of Alexandria. According to a fifth-century Byzantine historian named Socrates, she "far surpassed the other philosophers of her time,"[32]

(Bottom) A school scene from an ancient Greek vase. The Byzantines valued education and modeled the empire's schools on their Greek predecessors' examples. Teachers like the fifth-century Hypatia (top) were vital to the system.

A frenzied mob drags Hypatia through the streets to her death. Despite her fame and academic accomplishments, she was murdered for her pagan beliefs.

writing on a variety of subjects, such as astronomy, solid geometry, and arithmetic.

Hypatia liked to lecture about Plato and Aristotle on street corners, to any who would listen, and her fame was such that her students came from all over the empire. She still held to the old Greek and Roman gods, however, and because of her pagan beliefs, this distinguished scholar was brutally murdered in her mid-forties by a gang of fanatics.

Byzantine Literature

Byzantine education had a major weakness, its heavy dependence on the classical past and the Christian present. This dependence put strict limits on original thinking, and during their thousand-year history, the Byzantines produced little that was new in philosophy, mathematics, or science.

Their literature was almost as limited. As original writers, the Byzantines were noteworthy only for histories and religious works. Histories, such as those of the sixth-century writer Procopius, were immensely popular. According to the scholar Steven Runciman:

> To judge from the number of histories . . . and popular chroniclers and the frequent editions of the chronicles, [history] was . . . of widespread interest. The Byzantines loved to read of the past glories of the Empire; and the best-liked of the chronicles even stretched back to the Creation and Adam and Eve, and included the Tale of Troy. Past Emperors and past saints were vivid before their eyes.[33]

Religious Writings

Religious works, both books and hymns, were even more popular and successful than histories. For the better educated Byzantines, complicated books about religious theory were produced by such famous writers as Leontius of Byzantium and Maximus the Confessor. At their best,

Byzantine Frontiersman

The Byzantines had at least one folk hero, Basil Digenes Akritas, a cross between Davy Crockett and Sir Lancelot. This excerpt from the epic poem Digenes Akrites *appears in* Byzantine Heroic Poetry.

"The wonderful Basil, . . .
heard of raiders noble and valiant [brave]
. . . and zeal [enthusiasm] to see the raiders
    came over him
. . . He found . . . Philopappous . . .
'Welcome, young man . . . '
And then the youth . . . replied:
'. . . I am seeking and asking to become a raider myself'
. . . And . . . Philopappous thus replied:
. . . 'Young man if you boast of becoming a raider,
can you take your staff and go on an ambush,
and . . . for a fortnight [two weeks] . . .
not eat, not drink—not have fill of sleep—
and then roar like a lion so that the lions come
    out, and take their hides and bring them to me here?
. . . can you go on ambush
as lords are passing by with groom and bride
and all their army—and you go in the midst of them
and take the newly-wed bride and bring her to me here?'
And the Digenes spoke thus:
'. . . these things . . . I could do them at the age of five.
. . . if a stream
were . . . a mile in breadth [width],
even with feet together I could jump it in a trice
    [instant];
and overtake the hare three times even on sloping
    ground; and put out my hand and catch the
    partridge when it is flying low.'
And then Philopappous spoke thus:
'Draw up a silver stool, that master Basil may sit.'"

these works plunged their readers deep into the mysteries of the religion. At their worst, they were mere scorecards, toting up the points made by each writer in the endless debates about religious issues.

Even well-educated readers often found themselves lost in these works of religious theory, while the average citizen found such writings completely unapproachable and boring. Most Byzantine readers wanted something simpler and more dramatic, and they found it in the lives of anchorites, stylites, and saints.

Saints' lives were inspirational reading about the trials that holy men and women endured for their faith. These works described hardship, peril, and suffering and always ended with a victory for virtue and holiness. Many stories were fiction and openly labeled so, but they were just as popular as the stories that were said to be factual.

Prose works of other sorts were rare and of little importance. Although the Byzantines loved religious biographies, they had little taste for actual firsthand accounts of people's lives. Thus, few autobiographies or memoirs were produced. Fiction, except for tales about saints' lives, was practically unknown, being confined to some stories built around legends imported from India. Some minor poetry was produced, most of it a pale imitation of classical Greek and Roman work.

Stories about the lives of saints, such as St. Paul (shown here preaching), were the most popular form of Byzantine literature. The average Byzantine reader found the tales of their struggles and their triumphs inspiring.

Byzantine Architecture

Cramped though it was in other areas, Byzantine creativity did find an outlet. It blossomed in art, which blended together all the Greek, Roman, Near Eastern, and Christian elements that made up Byzantine culture.

Of all the Byzantine arts, architecture was the greatest, with original Byzantine architecture beginning during the reign of the sixth-century emperor Justinian I. After a massive Blues-Greens riot in 532, whole sections of Constantinople were left as fire-blackened ruins. Justinian soon launched a massive rebuilding program. The emperor did not want copies of the destroyed buildings, however, he wanted something new and better. Out of this desire on Justinian's part came building designs that, although owing something to the Roman past and the Near Eastern present, were distinctly Byzantine.

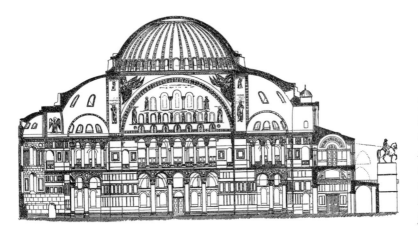

This cross-sectional view of Santa Sophia reveals the detail that architects Anthemius and Isidorus put into the project. The well-built church became a model for Muslim as well as Christian places of worship.

The Church of Santa Sophia

Justinian's chief architects were Anthemius of Tralles and Isidorus of Miletos, whose most famous project was the Church of Hagia Sophia, better known as the Church of Santa Sophia. The architects took the Roman basilica, a building shaped like a cross, and combined it with the dome, popular in the Near East. As the writer L. Sprague de Camp describes the church:

> The central part covered an area 120 feet square. At each corner of this square rose a huge 100-foot stone pier [column]. These piers in turn supported four arches, each 60 feet high. The arches upheld a dome . . . flattened at the top. On the east and west sides of the square, half-domes supported by semicircular walls buttressed [braced] the structure. . . . The inside was partitioned by arcades [balconies] mounted on rows of columns. . . . Most of the ornate decoration was inside . . . ; the outside was left functionally bare.[34]

Ten thousand workers labored over five years, and the result awed visitors to Constantinople. Even the worldly Byzantines were amazed by Santa Sophia. The Byzantine writer Procopius wrote that "one feels at once that it is the work not of man's effort . . . , but . . . the work of the divine power; and the spirit . . . realizes that here God is very near."[35]

Anthemius and Isidorus built well, for Santa Sophia still stands today, having survived fifteen hundred years of earthquakes, wars, riots, and fires. The domed roof introduced with Santa Sophia became a major feature of all Byzantine public buildings, and the dome plus basilica became the standard for Byzantine churches. It was quickly copied not only by other eastern churches but also by western European ones. In 1453, when Constantinople fell to the Ottoman Turks, the Muslim conquerors built their holy buildings along the same lines as Santa Sophia.

Mosaics and Other Arts

The Byzantines left the outside of their public buildings and churches bare, following the custom of keeping the outer walls of their homes undecorated. The interiors were extremely elaborate, however. The floors and walls were covered with mosaics, another of the great imperial arts. These mosaics were pictures made up of hundreds, sometimes thousands, of colored marble or glass cubes. Marble was

---

The Church of Santa Sophia

In this excerpt from Buildings, *quoted in* The Eagle, the Crescent, and the Cross, *the Byzantine historian Procopius describes the breathtaking Church of Santa Sophia, completed in 537.*

"The church has become a spectacle of marvelous beauty, overwhelming to those who see it. . . . For it soars to a height to match the sky. . . .

It . . . abounds [swarms] . . . in sunlight . . . in the reflection of the sun's rays from the marble. Indeed, one might say its interior is not illuminated [lit] from without by the sun, but that the radiance comes from within it. . . .

The whole ceiling is overlaid with pure gold, which adds glory to the beauty, yet the light reflected from the stone prevails, shining out in rivalry with the gold. And there are two . . . colonnades [balconies], one on each side . . . and reaching along its [the church's] whole length. . . . [T]hey . . . have . . . decorations of gold. One of these . . . colonnades has been assigned to men worshippers, while the other is reserved for women. . . . [W]ho could recount [describe] the beauty of the columns and the stones with which the church is adorned? . . . For he would surely marvel at the purple of some, the green tint of others, and at those on which the crimson glows and those from which the white flashes, and again at those which . . . [vary] with the most contrasting colors."

A modern view of Santa Sophia; its magnificence has awed people for nearly fifteen hundred years.

The completion of this mosaic, covering the inside of a church dome, was a painstaking process. Thousands of colored glass cubes, some as small as a pinhead, were set by hand one by one into the soft plaster of the ceiling.

used for floors and glass for the walls, with both coming in many colors.

The glass cubes, some of them backed with gold leaf, ranged from the size of a pinhead to an inch across, the smaller being used for fine detailed work such as eyes and the larger for bigger regions such as the picture's background. Byzantine artists then set each cube, one at a time, into damp plaster, which held everything in place when the composition dried.

Eventually, wall mosaics gave way to wall paintings, but in either case, the subject was most often religious. Naturally, pictures in churches depicted religious scenes, but so did many of those in government and other nonchurch buildings. Mosaics and paintings were generally of Christ, the Virgin Mary, or one of the many Byzantine saints.

The figures in Byzantine religious art are shown front forward, a convention the artists picked up from the Near East; the faces are distorted, with very large eyes, very much like those found in ancient Egyptian portraits. Also copied are the ancient Greek practices of painting the figures in robes and covering the backgrounds with drapes, (see the cover illustration), both of which indicate that indoor scenes are depicted.

Besides mosaics and wall paintings, other art forms flourished in the Byzantine Empire. Among these were gold and silver working, ivory carving, and weaving. Sculpture was favored by many emperors, who ordered statues of themselves, but it made the Christian Byzantines uncomfortable, since any statue, particularly a religious one, seemed to them like an idol.

Chapter

5 Riots, Laws, and Conquest

The emperor Justinian I was among the great sponsors of Byzantine architecture and art—one of his construction projects was the Church of Santa Sophia. But Justinian was more than just a builder of churches and public buildings. During his long reign from 527 to 565, he also standardized imperial law and reconquered parts of the former western Roman Empire.

Justinian I

Unlike most of the preceding emperors, Justinian was not an aristocrat. Indeed, the emperor was born in 482 to peasant parents near Sardica, deep in the Balkan peninsula and several hundred miles northwest of Constantinople. His origins may explain why as emperor, though he loved pomp and ceremony, he was also approachable: "for even men of low estate and altogether obscure had complete freedom not only to come before him but to converse with him." [36]

His uncle, Justin I, had been the commander of the palace guard, and when Emperor Anastasius I died in 518, Justin campaigned successfully to be named the new Byzantine ruler. Justin had already

brought Justinian to Constantinople, where the youth was educated before spending several years in the army. Justin I was an old man and preferred play to work. He thus put his ambitious and intel-

Justinian I's peasant upbringing may have enabled him to remain sympathetic to the commoners, who were allowed to visit and speak with him.

ligent nephew to managing the empire. By the time Justin I died in 527, Justinian was already an experienced imperial administrator.

Justinian's experience, combined with intelligence and a craving for hard work, made him a very capable ruler. He typically put in long days, beginning at dawn and running late into the night. In addition to his regular duties, the emperor found time to study law, architecture, music, poetry, religion, and philosophy. As historian Will Durant writes, "his mind was constantly active, equally at home in large designs and minute details."[37]

The Empress Theodora

In running the empire, Justinian I had the valuable help of his wife and empress, Theodora. Like her husband, Theodora was not a member of the aristocracy, her father having been a bear trainer and she herself an actress and dancer.

This past did not prevent her from becoming one of the most powerful people in the Byzantine Empire. She was intelligent, witty, and ambitious, with a good head for politics. Her husband recognized her abilities and made her the virtual co-ruler of the empire, saying that he took "as a participant in the decision [of managing the empire] my . . . consort [wife], given me by God."[38]

Because Justinian belonged to the Blues and Theodora to the Greens, the two often found themselves working toward different ends. At one time, Anthemius, the patriarch of Constantinople, refused to obey Justinian. The emperor exiled the patriarch from the city, but the

Empress Theodora's intelligence and ability earned her a position nearly as powerful as that of her husband, Justinian, but their differing political opinions often put them at odds.

empress, feeling that the sentence was unjust, hid Anthemius in her apartment for two years while she tried to have the exile canceled. Failing in her efforts, Theodora sent Anthemius into exile. She installed him in her palace across the Bosporus, which was only two miles from Constantinople. Still, no matter how difficult Theodora's plotting made Justinian's work, the emperor accepted it with good grace and patience.

A mosaic of Theodora and her attendants. Theodora's advice helped Justinian to keep his throne after he angered two political parties to the point of rioting.

The Nika Riot

It was Theodora who saved Justinian during the greatest crisis of his emperorship, the Nika riot of 532. During a rare moment of cooperation between the Blues and Greens, Justinian managed to anger both parties, thus setting off rioting. Tens of thousands of people rampaged through the city streets, killing police and other government officials, and burning down many public buildings. As the rioters wrecked the city, they shouted "Nika," the Greek word for "victory."

According to the Byzantine historian Procopius, only Theodora shamed Justinian into abandoning a plan to flee the city, and thus lose his throne, with the following speech:

My [Theodora's] opinion is that now . . . is a bad time to flee, even if this should bring safety. . . . [F]or a man who has been an Emperor to become a refugee is not to be borne. May I never be separated from the purple [the imperial color] and may I no longer live on that day when those who meet me shall not call me mistress. Now if you wish to save yourself, O Emperor, this is not hard. For we have much money; there is the sea, here are the boats. But think whether after you have been saved you may not come to feel that you would have preferred to die. As for me, I like a certain old proverb that says: royalty is a good shroud [burial garment].[39]

Justinian stayed. First, he had one of his aides bribe the leaders of the Blues to desert to the Greens. Then, the general Belisarius trapped most of the Green rioters in the Constantinople Hippodrome and killed some thirty thousand of them, ending the riot. Such wholesale butchery was not questioned at the time, since Byzantine rulers rarely showed mercy toward their enemies.

Reforming the Law

Thus, by following Theodora's advice, Justinian saved his crown. After the Nika riot, he ordered the rebuilding of the badly damaged city and turned to one of his

The Law of Justinian I

One of the major goals of Emperor Justinian I was to reform the Byzantine legal code. In this excerpt, quoted from The Eagle, the Crescent, and the Cross, *the emperor instructs the head of his law commission on the committee's duties.*

"We order you to read and revise the books relating to the Roman law drawn up by the jurists [judges] of antiquity . . . so that all the substance [of these books] may be collected, and . . . there shall remain no laws either similar to or inconsistent with one another, . . . [and] that there may be compiled from them a summary which will take the place of all. . . .

You shall divide the entire law into fifty books . . .; and that all the ancient law which has been in a confused condition for almost fourteen hundred years shall be embraced [contained] in the said fifty books. . . . All legal authors shall possess equal authority, and no preference shall be given to any, because all of them are neither superior nor inferior to one another. . . .

By no means do We allow you to insert . . . laws that appearing in ancient works have now fallen into desuetude [disuse]; since We only desire that legal procedure to prevail which has been most frequently employed, or which long custom has established. . . .

We desire . . . [that] no person learned in the law shall dare hereafter to add any commentaries . . ., and to confuse by . . . abridgement [shortening] of the aforesaid work, as was done in former times."

great interests, reform of the Byzantine legal code.

Imperial law was a mixture of the civic laws of Rome, the individual laws of each imperial region, rulings by judges, and imperial decrees. The code was so confusing that no one understood it. Justinian wanted to end this confusion and to produce a unified, official version of the code. As the emperor wrote:

We [Justinian] have found the entire arrangement of the law which has come down to us from the foundation of the City of Rome . . . to be so confused that it is . . . not within the grasp of human capacity [understanding]; and . . . We . . . begin by examining what had been enacted by former . . . princes, to correct their constitutions [laws], and make them more easily understood.[40]

The Code of Justinian

Justinian appointed a famous lawyer, Tribonian, to head a commission of ten legal experts to study the Byzantine laws. After having read two thousand books of law, Tribonian and his fellow commissioners produced a new legal code, the *Codex Justinianus*, or Code of Justinian, which in 529 replaced the earlier imperial code. Later, the code was expanded to include decrees by Justinian. To help law students in their study of the code, Tribonian also wrote a textbook, the *Institutes*.

In addition to the code, the commission assembled all the rulings, or opinions, of earlier Roman and Byzantine judges. These opinions were to be used in making judgments in new cases. Tribonian and the others were very selective in this collection. They included only opinions that did not challenge the authority of the emperor, and where necessary, they changed wording to achieve this end. Also, they altered some rulings to bring them into line with Christian doctrine and teachings.

Eventually, all the commission's work was published as the Body of Civil Law, although still known as the Code of Justinian. Whereas the original Code of Justinian had been in Latin, the final code was written in Greek, which remained the

Justinian hands his legal code to the lawyer Tribonian, who had led a team of experts and studied numerous law books to produce it.

The Code of Justinian was originally written in Latin, as this section is, and was later translated into Greek. A basic tenet of the code was that all law comes from the emperor and must concur with Christian belief.

official language of imperial law until the empire's end in the fifteenth century.

The Nature of the Code

The Code of Justinian was in many ways a blueprint of Byzantine society. It was rooted in two concepts: first, that all law comes from the emperor and, second, that all law must be based on orthodox, that is, officially accepted, Christianity.

The code ruled that citizens, those born free, were either persons of rank or commoners. It recognized slavery, and although it encouraged the freeing of slaves, it allowed desperately poor parents to sell newborn children into slavery. It created a class of serfs by ordering that any farmer who remained on his land for more than thirty years had to stay there permanently, as did his children. Serfs who left without their landlord's permission could be returned just like runaway slaves.

Justinian (pictured) created laws that allowed women to inherit property and divorce their husbands, but the code also recognized slavery and allowed torturous physical punishments for some crimes.

The code, however, also provided protection for some individual rights, particularly when it came to inheritance and property. Under Justinian's laws, a woman could inherit property, and if her husband died, she could assume the guardianship of her children. Women were also no longer subject to the death penalty if they committed adultery, although men were. Rape was a capital crime, and the rapist's property was confiscated and given to his victim.

Initially, the only reason for divorce recognized in the code was the entrance of a husband or wife into a monastery or a convent. However, many vocal protests brought a number of additional grounds for divorce into the code. Divorce by mutual consent was not part of the code until after Justinian's death; but during his lifetime, a wife, for example, could divorce her husband if he was unfaithful, if he accused her falsely of adultery, or if he kept her captive.

Trial and Punishment

Under the Code of Justinian, a person accused of a crime could be thrown into prison only by the order of a judge. Trials had to follow within a set time after imprisonment and had to be conducted by a judge appointed by the emperor. Lawyers had to swear on a Bible that they would defend their clients well, while their clients had to swear to the justice of their cases.

Defendants who were found guilty faced a host of penalties. They might be fined or lose part or all of their property. Even harsher punishments existed, although trial judges could show leniency and order a lesser penalty. For instance, crooked tax collectors or heretics who wrote about Monophysitism could lose a hand. Other offenders had their noses cut off, while still others were blinded. Various crimes called for death by beheading, crucifixion, or burning alive. Gay men could expect death after torture, mutilation, and public display; lesbians, however, were ignored by the code.

Justinian's code would eventually be copied by other European societies during the Renaissance, and it remains part of many legal codes in Europe to this day. The scholar Aikaterina Christophilopoulou writes that "Justinian's monumental work of codifying the laws . . . formed the foundation of later European codes. . . . [I]t is the book that has had the greatest repercussions [effects] on mankind after the Bible."[41]

Foreign Wars

At the same time that Justinian was reforming the Byzantine legal code, he was engaged in a series of wars of conquest, first against North Africa, then Italy, and finally Spain. The emperor badly wanted to restore the full boundaries of the old Roman Empire. He failed to do so; but still, under him, the Byzantine Empire in 554 reached its greatest extent.

Justinian's wars were expensive, and the emperor quickly used up the 320,000 pounds of gold that had been in the imperial treasury when he took the throne. He then had to resort to heavy and unpopular taxes to keep his army in the field.

Pay for the army was one of Justinian's biggest worries. The imperial army was made up of mercenaries, who came from all over the empire, Europe, and the Near East. Like all mercenaries, they were costly, and often they were unreliable. These imperial troops sometimes mutinied during battles, and they lost more than one fight by stopping to loot rather than pursuing the enemy. Regular pay made them more manageable and less prone to impulsive looting.

General Belisarius

Byzantine soldiers were also more reliable when led by a good general. Justinian found such a commander in Belisarius, who had so successfully crushed the Nika riot. Like Justinian, Belisarius was of peasant stock, born in what would become

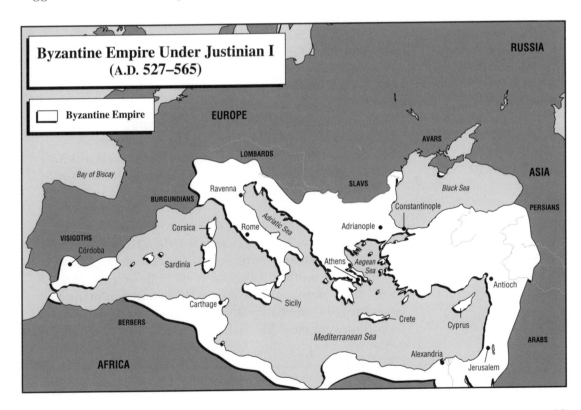

Byzantine Empire Under Justinian I
(A.D. 527–565)

☐ **Byzantine Empire**

RUSSIA

EUROPE

AVARS

ASIA

LOMBARDS

SLAVS

Black Sea

Bay of Biscay

BURGUNDIANS

Ravenna

Constantinople

PERSIANS

VISIGOTHS

Corsica

Rome

Adriatic Sea

Adrianople

Córdoba

Sardinia

Athens

Aegean Sea

Antioch

Carthage

Sicily

Crete

Cyprus

BERBERS

Mediterranean Sea

ARABS

AFRICA

Alexandria

Jerusalem

western Bulgaria. He was one of the greatest of the empire's many generals, winning more battles than any other Byzantine commander of his day.

Belisarius equipped his soldiers with good weapons and armor, an action that had much to do with his great success.

Each of his elite troops carried a lance, a long sword, and a bow, and each wore a scale-mail coat. From this beginning grew the uniformly equipped and trained Byzantine army that would be the most powerful military force in Europe for centuries to come.

Textbook for Byzantine Law Students

In 533 Tribonian, who had headed the legal reform committee of Emperor Justinian I, prepared a detailed summary to explain the empire's legal code to law students, the Institutes. *It is excerpted here from* Medieval Europe: A Short Sourcebook.

"1. Civil law . . . and the law of nations . . . are divided in this way. . . . The law that each people has established for itself is particular [special] to that state and is called civil law. . . . [W]hat natural reason has established among all men is kept equally by all peoples and is called the law of nations. . . . [T]he Roman people [the Byzantines] observe partly their own particular law [and] partly that which is common to all peoples. . . .

3. Our law is derived from [comes from] written or unwritten [sources]. . . .

4. A 'law'. . . is that which the Roman people commanded on a question submitted by a senatorial magistrate. . . .

6. The emperor's voice has the force of law . . . since, by the 'law of kings'. . . which regulated his authority . . ., the people conceded [gave] to him and placed in him all their power and authority. Thus, whatever the emperor directed . . . or decreed [ordered] . . . is to be . . . law. . . .

9. Unwritten law is that which usage has approved, for long-observed customs take on the effect of law by consent [agreement] of those who observe them. . . .

11. And, natural laws, which are followed by all nations alike, deriving from divine providence, remain always firm and unchangeable; . . . those which each state constitutes [makes] for itself [are] often subject to alteration [change]."

it lasted, it tied up troops that he wanted to use in his reconquest of the west. Finally, Justinian made peace by buying it, promising a yearly payment to Persia of eleven thousand pounds of gold.

Conquest of North Africa

Despite having sworn with the Persian ruler to the Everlasting Peace of 532, Justinian would find himself at war with Persia twice more, in 540 and 549. However, for the moment, he could turn his attention to the west, and the old lands of the western Roman Empire.

In June 533, Belisarius sailed for Carthage in North Africa, which had been overrun by the German Vandals a century before. Despite being outnumbered, Belisarius's eighteen thousand soldiers easily defeated the Vandals in two major battles. The Vandals, who had been a fearsome menace in the fifth century, had declined militarily and were no match for the imperial troops, trained and armed by Belisarius and hardened by their recent war with Persia. North Africa was once more under the rule of an emperor.

Invasion of Italy

Justinian's next target was the Ostrogothic kingdom in Italy. The Byzantine invasion began in 536 and at first went well. Belisarius quickly captured Sicily and then crossed to the mainland, moving up southern Italy to Rome. The Ostrogoths were politically divided, and their resistance was light. The imperial army

Belisarius, one of the most famous and capable Byzantine generals, conquered old parts of the Roman Empire, stretching the borders of the Byzantine Empire to their fullest extent.

War with Persia

Before Justinian could launch his wars of conquest, he had to end a war with the Persian Empire that had broken out in 527. The two empires were ancient enemies and shared a long border. Relations were always uneasy and occasionally broke down completely, leading to war.

After five years of warfare, during which Belisarius won one major battle and lost another, neither side was close to a definitive victory. Justinian became impatient with this never-ending war. As long as

By this time, Byzantine reinforcements had arrived to support Belisarius. Fighting continued for three years, however, before Witigis surrendered. Rivalry and friction between Belisarius and another imperial general, Narses, led to "a . . . row [argument] . . . in the Roman headquarters, [where] operations were launched and cancelled, and backbiting and intrigue became the order of the day."[42] This feuding ended with the destruction of an imperial garrison and much of the town of Milan in 539. Narses was recalled to Constantinople, and the next year, Belisarius took Ravenna by pretending to accept the Goths' offer to become their king.

The Fall of Rome

Belisarius returned to Constantinople to celebrate his Italian victories. However, three years later, news came that the Ostrogoths, under a new leader, had recaptured Rome and other Italian cities. Belisarius returned immediately to Italy, where he eventually retook Rome. However, Rome was to change hands twice more, and years of fighting were to pass, before the Goths were driven from Italy in 552 by Belisarius's one-time imperial rival, Narses.

After more than fifteen years of war, even the remains of the western Roman Empire were gone. Rome itself was wrecked more thoroughly by this war than by all the earlier barbarian raids combined. The other sections of the western empire, such as Gaul, remained forever outside the Byzantine Empire because the government in Constantinople had no resources left to conquer them. Only

Belisarius brings captive Vandals and booty before Emperor Justinian after a crushing victory. The defeat of the Vandals in 533 brought North Africa under Byzantine rule.

marched into Rome unopposed, the citizens cheering Belisarius as their liberator.

Meanwhile, the Ostrogoths, under a new king, Witigis, drew all their forces together and surrounded Rome. Belisarius had 5,000 men with which to defend the city from 150,000 Goths. Despite the overwhelming odds against them, the Byzantine soldiers held the city, and after a year, the Goths retreated to their capital of Ravenna.

Belisarius in Italy

When the Byzantine general Belisarius invaded Italy in 536, he found himself surrounded in Rome by a large army of Ostrogoths and wrote Emperor Justinian I for help, as reported in Procopius's History of the Wars, *quoted here from Robert Browning's* Justinian and Theodora.

"We have appointed [ordered] a large part of the soldiers to garrison [staff] forts in Sicily and Italy, . . . and [all] we have left [is] an army of only five thousand. The enemy are coming against us to the number of one hundred and fifty thousand. . . . [W]e were forced . . . to come to grips with them, and . . . we were nearly buried beneath the multitude of their spears. Later, when the barbarians made an attempt on the [city] wall with their entire army . . ., they came very near to taking us and the city at first blow. . . . Thus far we have done well . . .; but . . . let weapons and soldiers be sent to us in sufficient quantities to establish us in future in this war on a basis of equality with our enemies. . . . [I]f the barbarians defeat us now, we shall be driven out of your Italy and lose the army as well, and in addition shall bear the great shame of our failure. . . . [W]e should give [would be giving] the impression of having abandoned the citizens of Rome, who have thought less of their safety than of their loyalty to your empire. And so even our successes will turn out but the prelude [introduction] to disaster."

Belisarius prepares to leave Constantinople to conquer Italy, a territory occupied by the Ostrogoths. The trip resulted in a three-year battle for control of Italy, a struggle in which the Byzantines eventually prevailed.

southern Spain was occupied by Byzantine troops for a time. So, the fall of Rome, which had begun in the fifth century, was completed by the middle of the sixth. The Roman Empire was shattered forever.

Justinian and Belisarius

Belisarius's success in war earned him the personal loyalty of his troops, and the admiration of the citizens of Constantinople. As Procopius writes:

> [The people] took delight in watching Belisarius as he came forth from his home each day. . . . For his progress resembled a crowded festival procession, since he was always escorted by a large number of Vandals . . . [and] Goths. . . . Furthermore, he had a fine figure, and was tall and remarkably handsome. But his conduct was so meek, and his manners so affable [friendly] that he seemed like a very poor man, and one of no repute [fame].[43]

Belisarius's fame led Justinian to distrust the general. Popular commanders had seized thrones in the past, and Justinian feared that Belisarius had the same intention. Thus, in 548, the same year that Theodora died, Justinian recalled Belisarius for the last time and forced him into retirement.

For all Justinian's suspicions, Belisarius never gave any hint that he had designs

Narses leads the Byzantine army as they drive the Ostrogoths out of Italy. The victory in 552 ended years of fighting with the Goths.

Justinian, depicted on horseback in this ivory carving, suspected that Belisarius wanted to take the throne from him. Justinian's suspicions led him to force the general into retirement and confiscate half of his property when he died.

on the imperial throne. He remained loyal to Justinian and the empire. In 559, as an old man, he took a few hundred troops and routed an invading force of seven thousand Huns that had besieged Constantinople. Because he did not pursue the fleeing barbarians, however, the Byzantine commander was suspected of treachery. On the basis of this and past suspicions, the emperor confiscated half the general's property when Belisarius died in 565. A few months later, Justinian was also dead of old age.

Justinian I left the Byzantine Empire with a new legal code and a vastly larger territory. He also left it with an empty treasury and an exhausted army. It would prove increasingly difficult for the emperors who immediately followed him to govern and to protect this enlarged empire.

6 Slavs, Avars, Persians, and Muslims

Upon the death of Justinian I in 565, the Byzantine Empire was the largest and most powerful state in Europe. It was rich with trade, rich with culture, yet within fifty years, it would teeter on the brink of disaster, much of its land in the hands of first one invader and then another.

The Legacy of Justinian I

The empire's troubles arose directly out of the reign of Justinian I. First, Justinian had left the empire in deep financial trouble. During his many years on the throne, the Byzantines were almost always at war. It took a lot of money to buy the supplies and arms and to meet the payrolls for four decades of war.

On top of the war expenses were the costs of Justinian's ambitious rebuilding of Constantinople after the Nika revolt in 532. The Church of Santa Sophia alone cost 320,000 pounds of gold, which was the amount the imperial treasury had held when Justinian came to power. And Santa Sophia was only one of dozens of buildings the emperor sponsored.

At Justinian's death, the Byzantine government was close to broke. The next three emperors, Justin II, Tiberius II, and Maurice, barely kept the empire afloat by heavily taxing Byzantine citizens.

Second, Justinian had left the empire with a military crisis. The Byzantine army was scattered all over the newly expanded empire. Many units were tied up fighting in Africa against fierce nomads called Berbers, and in Italy against the Lombards, a Germanic tribe, who had successfully taken much of the empire's land in northern Italy. The remainder of the army formed a thin line of defense that was too fragile to protect the imperial borders. The empire was open to attack, and that attack was not long in coming.

The Slavs and the Avars

To the north of Constantinople, the Byzantine Empire's Balkan territory was being raided by a new group of barbarians, the Slavs. To stop these raids, which began in 550, the Byzantines arranged with the Avars, a people related to the Huns, to attack the Slavs. The empire hoped that the Slavs would be so busy fighting the Avars that they would not have time for raiding the Balkans.

The plan misfired badly, as large armies of Slavs, fleeing the Avars, drove

Revolution in Constantinople

Over the next two decades, the imperial government did its best to stop the Avars. However, Emperor Maurice received little support from the imperial citizenry. Thousands of Byzantines fled to monasteries to escape military service. In 602 Maurice ordered the monasteries to close their doors to new members until the threat posed by the Avars was over. The emperor's action enraged the monks, who with the aid of the Blues and Greens, prodded the people into revolting against Maurice.

While the rebels rioted in Constantinople, the army fighting the Avars mutinied, "being worn out and dispirited at the prospect of a war whose end was not in sight."[44] After killing their senior officers and choosing an illiterate junior officer, Phocas, as their leader, the army marched on the capital and joined forces with the Blues and the Greens. Maurice and his family were killed, and Phocas became the new emperor.

War with Persia

Justinian I, shown here, left the Byzantine Empire financially exhausted and vulnerable to foreign attack.

deep into the Balkans, occasionally threatening Constantinople itself. Many Slavs ended up staying and occupying the Balkan peninsula. Further, in 582, the Avars turned on the Byzantines and began attacking the Balkans with armies composed of conquered Slavs.

To the east, the Persians took advantage of the confusion caused by the Byzantine revolution and hit the empire hard, driving deep into imperial territory. Taking almost all available army units, Phocas counterattacked, but he was unable to stop the Persians, who in 602 began grabbing off large chunks of the Byzantine state, which would eventually include Syria and Egypt. The recent revolution of citizens and soldiers had so sapped the energies and resources of the empire that it could not defend itself.

Meanwhile, Phocas's unsuccessful campaign against the eastern enemy had stripped away so many troops from the Balkans that the Avars were able to march far into Byzantine territory, even capturing farmland near Constantinople. The Byzantine Empire appeared doomed.

Heraclius's New Army

In 610, when Byzantine fortunes were at their lowest, Heraclius, son of the military commander of Africa, killed Phocas and seized the throne. It took the new emperor ten hard years to renew "the morale of the people, the strength of the army, and the resources of the treasury."[45]

Constantinople (bottom), with its strong defenses, remained secure as the Avars and Persians invaded and conquered Byzantine territory. The empire was in a slump, both economically and militarily, when Heraclius (top) took the throne and set out to rebuild the empire.

Treaty with Persia

The Byzantine and Persian Empires fought each other in many wars, and they signed a number of peace treaties. This excerpt from The History of Menander the Guardsman, *translated by R. C. Blockley, is an example of such a treaty and shows that the concerns of these ancient states were much the same as those of modern nations.*

"1. The Persians shall not allow . . . barbarians [any non-Persians such as Arabs] access to the Roman Empire, nor shall the Romans either in that area or any other part of the Persian frontier send an army against Persia. . . .

3. Roman and Persian merchants of all kinds of goods . . . shall conduct their business . . . through the . . . custom posts.

4. Ambassadors and all others using the public post [roads] to deliver messages, both those traveling to Roman and those to Persian territory, shall be honored . . . and shall receive the appropriate attention. . . .

5. It is agreed that Saracen [Arab] and all other barbarian merchants of either state . . . shall not cross into foreign territory without official permission. . . .

6. If anyone during the period of hostilities defected either from the Romans to the Persians or from the Persians to the Romans and if he should give himself up and wish to return home, he shall not be prevented from so doing. . . . But those who in time of peace defect . . . shall not be received, but every means shall be used to return them. . . .

7. Those who complain that they have suffered some hurt at the hands of subjects of the other state shall settle the dispute equitably [fairly], meeting at the border . . . and in this manner the guilty party shall make good the damage."

One of Heraclius's first actions was to rebuild the army. He established in Asia Minor military districts called themes. Each theme's commander was also the area's civilian governor, and its soldiers doubled as farmers. The theme system made for a far better and far more reliable army, since the empire no longer had to depend on expensive and untrustworthy mercenaries. As the historian Crane Brinton writes:

In each theme the troops were recruited from the native population; in return for their services, . . . [they] were granted land but they were not allowed to dispose of it or to evade their duties as soldiers. Their sons

Sword poised over his head, Heraclius prepares to kill a Persian enemy leader, whose crown falls to the ground. Heraclius's army reconquered land lost to the Persians.

He . . . had concentrated on the study of military science. . . . The use of cavalry in the Byzantine army became increasingly important, and Heraclius . . . attached special significance to the lightly-armed mounted archers. The real campaigning did not begin until the autumn.[47]

It was a long, difficult war, and at one point in 626, the Avars laid siege to Constantinople, while the Persians threatened the city from across the Bosporus. The imperial army first routed the Avars and then chased the Persians away.

After their defeat at Constantinople, the Avars were no longer a threat to the empire. Within two years, neither were the Persians. A combination of a Byzantine victory over the Persians in 627 that practically wiped out the enemy army and the overthrow of the Persian ruler a year later ended the war in 629.

Heraclius had regained all the territory lost to the Persians, and with war payments from the Persians and contributions from the wealthy Byzantine church, he refilled the imperial treasury. The empire seemed safe and stable once more. Then in 634, only five years after the Persian victory, a new enemy struck. Arabs, who were newly converted to Islam, the religion founded by the prophet Muhammad, stormed into Syria.

Islam was to become one of the world's great religions and a major force in the medieval world. Its followers, known as Muslims, had recently conquered all of Arabia, and now they turned their holy war, or jihad, against the Byzantine and Persian Empires.

Within three years the Byzantine Empire, the first European state to feel the

inherited the property along with the obligation to fight. . . . From the start, one of the themes was naval.[46]

In addition to the troops of the themes, the emperor had army and navy units of his own at Constantinople.

Winning Back the Empire

In the spring of 622, Heraclius set out to push the Persians back beyond the empire's eastern border. He went first to the themes of Asia Minor to collect and train the soldiers there. The scholar George Ostrogorsky relates

In Asia Minor [Heraclius] set out for the . . . themes, and here he got together his army and spent the entire summer training the fresh troops.

impact of the Islamic jihad, suffered major losses: Syria in 635 and Palestine, along with Jerusalem, in 637. In 641, the year Heraclius died, the Arabs took Egypt, and all the territories regained from Persia were once more lost, this time forever.

As the Arabs swept over the Byzantine Near East, they also crushed Persia, which fell to them in 641. The Byzantines suffered a further loss, with North Africa being overrun by Muslim armies in 698. Thus, by the end of the seventh century, the empire had lost almost all its land outside of western and central Asia Minor, the Balkans, and Italy.

The seventh-century jihad's success was helped greatly by two major factors. First, Heraclius's victory over Persia had been costly. Both the Byzantines and the Persians were drained by their years of war, and they were easy prey for the Muslim armies that burst out of Arabia in 634.

Second, when Heraclius had regained Egypt and Syria from the Persians, he had cracked down on the Jews and the Monophysites, the latter making up the bulk of the population of these imperial provinces. These groups saw the arrival of the Arabs, who did not persecute either Christians or Jews, as a way of escaping imperial harassment. To the Muslim Arabs, what was important was that both Christians and Jews believed in a single God and that they were "peoples of the Book," whether the book was the Koran, the collection of Islamic holy writings, or the Bible.

The Arabs' broad-mindedness came from more than just religious tolerance. It also served Muslim self-interest because Islamic states had a special tax for nonbelievers. Therefore, Muslim domains profited by not rushing conversions.

The Defense of Constantinople

No matter how successful the Arabs were militarily, they were not unbeatable. They tried twice to take Constantinople, with the goal of opening up a route into eastern Europe. They failed both times. The first attempt came in 674: the Arabs attacked by sea, and the imperial navy defeated them, setting the Muslim fleet aflame with Greek fire.

In 717 the Arabs made their final bid to take the Byzantine capital. Again they were repulsed, this time by the inspired defense of Emperor Leo III. As historian Will Durant writes:

> An army of 80,000 Arabs and Persians . . . besieged Constantinople from the rear. At the same time the Arabs fitted out a fleet of 1800 vessels . . . ; this armada entered the Bosporus. . . . It was the good fortune of the Greeks [the Byzantines] that . . . an able general Leo . . . [seized] the throne. . . . He disposed [positioned] the small Byzantine navy with . . . skill, and saw to it that every ship was well supplied with Greek fire. In a little while the Arab vessels were aflame, and nearly every ship in the great fleet was destroyed. The Greek army made a sortie [attack] upon the besiegers, and won so decisive a victory that . . . [the Muslims] withdrew to Syria.[48]

Defender of the West

Although it certainly was not the Byzantine Empire's intention, battling the Avars and more importantly, the Muslims, pro-

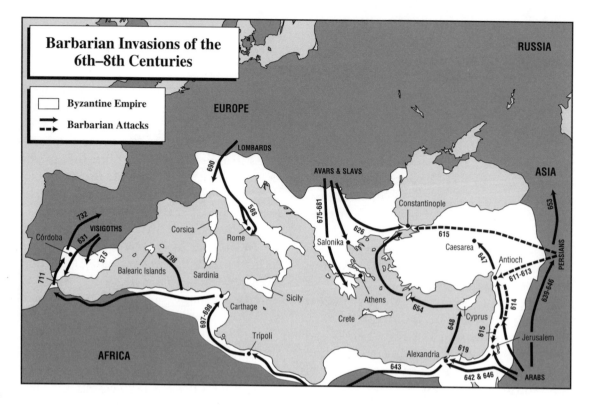

Barbarian Invasions of the 6th–8th Centuries

Byzantine Empire
Barbarian Attacks

RUSSIA

EUROPE

ASIA

LOMBARDS

690

AVARS & SLAVS

675-681

Constantinople

626

PERSIANS

653

732

VISIGOTHS

Corsica

Rome

568

Salonika

615

Caesarea

Antioch

647

611-613

639-646

Córdoba

631

575

Balearic Islands

798

Sardinia

711

Sicily

Athens

654

Cyprus

614

615

Jerusalem

697-698

Carthage

Crete

648

619

AFRICA

Tripoli

Alexandria

643

642 & 646

ARABS

tected western Europe from these invaders. Instead of spreading westward, the Avars turned south toward Constantinople. There, they wore themselves out in their unsuccessful attempts to capture the Byzantine capital.

The Muslims, too, slammed hard against the thus far unbreakable defenses of Constantinople. The historian George Ostrogorsky writes that "the Byzantine capital was the last dam left to withstand the rising Muslim tide. The fact that it held saved not only the Byzantine Empire, but the whole of European civilization."[49]

The only Muslim conquest in western Europe was that of the Visigothic kingdom of Spain. The remaining military energies of the Arabs went into their war with the Byzantine Empire, a war that eventually drained their will to continue fighting. By the end of the ninth century, the Arab states would no longer be as strong as they had been and would no longer pose a threat to Europe.

7 Bulgars, Heretics, and Landlords

Peace continued to elude the Byzantine Empire even after the end of Muslim expansion. The empire had to keep its eastern forces strong to discourage the Muslims, and it also had to fight the Slavs, who were now settled in the Balkans. At the same time, it was once more troubled by internal conflict caused by religious quarreling and by a shift in power from the emperor to powerful landholders.

The Byzantines and the Slavs

Throughout the eighth century, the empire adjusted to the permanent settlement of the Slavs in the Balkans. As the scholar George Ostrogorsky observes:

> During the . . . Byzantine period no [external] development . . . was of greater significance . . . than the Slav penetration into the Balkans. All other barbarian inroads into the Empire . . . were temporary . . . , and even the great Germanic invasions . . . finally moved elsewhere. The Slavs, however, made a permanent home in the Balkans, and the outcome of this penetration was . . . the later growth of . . . Slav kingdoms.[50]

The Byzantines' defeat of the Muslims at Constantinople in 674 impressed some of the Slavs deeply, and these barbarian tribes sent representatives to the emperor, accepting his authority. Still, on-again, off-again fighting continued with the remainder of the Slavs.

The Bulgars

Much of the fighting between Byzantines and Slavs arose from conflict with the Bulgarian Kingdom. Located in the northeast Balkans, this kingdom sprawled almost equally north and south of the Danube.

The Bulgar domain was the first Slav kingdom, although the Bulgars were not Slavs but Asian nomads who had entered the Balkans in 680. However, in the new kingdom large numbers of Slavs vastly outnumbered the Bulgars. During the next century, the two groups mixed so thoroughly that the Bulgar minority literally disappeared into the Slavic majority.

The Bulgarian Kingdom mounted numerous attacks on the Byzantine Empire, and in 811, Emperor Nicephorus I led an army north to deal with the barbarians. The outcome was a serious blow to the Byzantines: the Bulgars destroyed the

Symeon's Kingdom

**Bulgarian Kingdom
Under Symeon**

imperial troops and killed Nicephorus. Two years later, the Bulgars struck at Constantinople. Like other armies, however, the attackers failed to break through the city's defenses.

Byzantine Culture and the Slavs

After its failure to take Constantinople, the Bulgarian Kingdom established more peaceable relations with the empire. Byzantine traders found a good market in this and other Slavic kingdoms, selling the barbarians everything from crop seeds and plows to silk and gold jewelry. Byzantine architects even went north to design and erect buildings for Slavic rulers.

Byzantine teachers brought books and art to the Slavs, many of whose leaders were educated at Constantinople. Eventually, Slavic ways and customs gave way to Byzantine manners, and although the empire did not physically control the Slavic kingdoms, its influences created a Byzantine culture in them. As the scholar Steven Runciman writes:

> [The Bulgarian Kingdom] was a very Byzantine civilization. . . . Symeon [the ruler], . . . chief patron of the new culture, had been educated at Constantinople, where he read deep[ly]. . . . At his court translators flocked to render Greek chronicles, homilies [religious writings] and romances into the Slavonic; his buildings in his vast capital . . . copied . . . the splendors of Constantinople.[51]

In further imitation of the Byzantine state in 893, Symeon dubbed himself an emperor and the Bulgarian Kingdom an empire.

The Slavs and Christianity

Byzantine missionaries began converting the Slavs to Christianity in the ninth century, and religion became the Byzantine Empire's strongest tie to the barbarians. The Eastern Church also provided the Slavs with an alphabet. Known as Cyrillic lettering, this alphabet was created by the Byzantine missionary Cyril and is still used today in parts of eastern Europe and Russia.

In the conversion of the Slavs, which began in earnest in 864, the Byzantines found themselves competing with missionaries from the Roman Catholic Church. In the end, the Slavs were divided fairly evenly between the two branches of Catholicism. Each branch normally won over the Slavs who were closest to it geographically. Thus, the Byzantine church pulled in Slavs living in the central and eastern Balkans and Russia, while the Roman church took in Slavs in central Europe and the northwestern Balkans.

Serbia and Croatia

It was not unusual for neighboring Slavic kingdoms to belong to different branches of the church. For example, two Slavic kingdoms, Serbia and Croatia, were divided from each another because the Serbs had joined the Eastern Church and the Croats were Roman Catholic. The dif-

ferent Christian choices of the two kingdoms affected their relationship, and they became bitter rivals in the region.

These ancient rivalries are still very much alive today. The fighting that broke out in the former Yugoslavia began in 1990 when Croatia seceded, claiming that it had little in common with the Serb-dominated society. The new Yugoslav republic, consisting of Serbia and the former Montenegro, immediately sent its

The Byzantine missionary Cyril, pictured here, was influential in converting the Slavs in the eastern Balkans and Russia to the Byzantine church. He later became St. Cyril.

Byzantine emperor Leo III (left) forbade the worship of icons in 726. This enraged monks, whose supporters attacked the soldiers assigned to remove the statues and paintings.

Christ, and the various saints was sinful. Icons were to be found in almost every Byzantine church, monastery, shop, and house, and venerating was the act of honoring these objects in formal, religious-like ways.

The iconoclasts were upset because people seemed to take veneration to the extreme of worshiping icons, a practice that smacked of ancient pagan idol worship. The image breakers further supported their position by pointing to the second commandment, "Thou shalt not make unto thee any graven images," and the verses from the New Testament, saying that "God is spirit: and they that worship him must worship him in spirit."

Rioting and Repression

In 726 the Byzantine emperor Leo III forbade the use and display of icons. Again, an imperial act enraged the monasteries, whose monks were firmly attached to the practice of venerating icons. Egged on by angry monks, mobs attacked soldiers, who were assigned to remove icons from all public and religious buildings.

Civil war erupted when Greek rebels, favoring icons, declared their independence from Leo and Constantinople. Partisans on both sides called their opponents heretics. The rebels gathered together a fleet, which was sunk along with their cause by the imperial navy.

Leo's son, Constantine V, was also an iconoclast, and under him, the movement reached an all-time low. In 754, a church council packed with Constantine's supporters ruled against the veneration of icons. The emperor then launched a

army to assist Serbs who were living in Croatia and wanted to break away from the Croats. The Croatian Serbs believed that culturally they belonged with their fellow Serbs, not the Croats.

Iconoclasm

For the Byzantines, Balkan problems were often overshadowed by a new, bitter argument over what was acceptable Christian practice. Throughout much of the eighth century, imperial officials, from the emperor on down, as well as ordinary citizens, focused their attention on the latest religious controversy, iconoclasm.

Iconoclasm, which means the breaking of images, was a belief that the practice of venerating holy statues and painted images, or icons, of the Virgin Mary,

The Conflict over Images

In the eighth century, the Byzantines grappled with iconoclasm, whose followers claimed that the creation of icons, or holy images, led to idolatry. Both these excerpts are quoted in The Eagle, the Crescent, and the Cross, *the argument for images comes from a book written in 742 by St. John of Damascus (*The Fount of Wisdom) *and that against them comes from a decree issued by a church council that convened in 754.*

"Since some find fault with us for worshipping and honoring the image of our Savior and that of our Lady [the Virgin Mary], and those . . . of the . . . saints . . . , let them remember that . . . God created man after his own image. . . . [W]e shew [show] reverence to each other . . . because we are made after God's image. . . . [T]he honor given to the image passes over to the prototype. Now a prototype is that which is imaged. . . .

[The story of Christ was] written for the remembrance and instruction of us who were not alive at that time. . . . But seeing that not everyone has a knowledge of letters [can read] . . ., the [church] Fathers gave their sanction [permission] to depicting these events on images."

"God sent his own Son, who turned us away from . . . the worshipping of idols, and taught us the worshipping of God in spirit. . . . [The followers] of wickedness . . . gradually brought back idolatry [idol worship] under the appearance of Christianity. As Christ . . . armed his Apostles against the ancient idolatry . . . , so has he awakened against the new idolatry his servants our faithful Emperors. . . .

The painter, who . . . depicts that which should not be depicted . . . tries to fashion that which should be believed in the heart. . . . [H]e has . . . in his representation . . . depicted Godhead which cannot be represented."

Iconoclasts sweep through a Byzantine church, smashing images and statues of the Virgin Mary and Jesus, while worshipers weep and protest.

campaign of terror that destroyed thousands of icons and that led to the torture, mutilation, and death of their owners.

In 787, another church council was called by the Empress Irene. Irene, who was regent for her son Constantine VI, the grandson of Constantine V, approved of icon veneration, and the council she assembled did also, reversing the previous 754 ruling against icons.

After 800, although iconoclasm was restored by Leo V in 815, it played only a minor role in imperial politics. By 843, tempers on both sides had cooled and a final church council, under the emperor Michael III, ruled in favor of the proper use of religious images and thus put an end to iconoclasm.

More internal trouble, however, lay ahead for the empire. A new political group, known as the Powerful, arose during the last half of the ninth century. The Powerful were landholders who built huge estates, sometimes through the purchase of land, sometimes by means of theft. These landowners and the emperors were soon locked in a struggle for control of the Byzantine Empire.

The Macedonian

The imperial dynasty that fought with the Powerful was the Macedonian. The first Macedonian emperor was Basil I, who like Justinian I, had been born a peasant. In 843, at the age of twenty-five, having spent much of his youth as a Bulgar slave, Basil escaped and reached Constantinople. A capable and intelligent man, the former slave rose rapidly from diplomat's groom

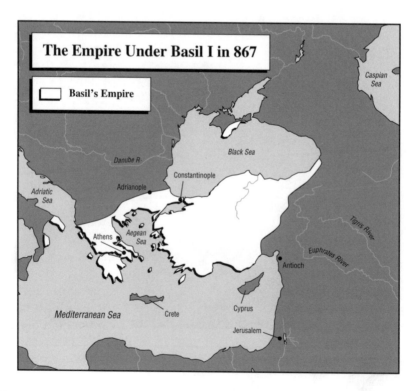

The Empire Under Basil I in 867

Basil's Empire

Indictment of the Powerful

In this indictment, quoted in A History of Civilization, *by Crane Brinton and others, the late-tenth-century emperor Basil II describes which of the mighty landowners, known as the Powerful, had become rich through stolen land.*

"Constantine Maleinos and his son . . . have for a hundred years . . . been in undisputed possession of lands unjustly acquired. It is the same with the Phocas family, who . . . , for more than a century, have also succeeded in holding onto lands wrongly obtained. In more recent times certain newly-rich men have done the same. For example, Philokales, a simple peasant who lived for a long while in poverty . . . and paid the same taxes as other peasants . . . , now has . . . [illegally] acquired vast estates. He has not gone unpunished. When we [Basil II] arrived in the region where his property is located, and heard the complaints of those whom he had dispossessed [robbed of land] we commanded that all the buildings he had built be razed [torn down] and that the lands ravished [stolen] from the poor be returned to them. Now this man is living again on the small piece of property which he owned at the start of his career, and has once more become what he was by birth, a simple peasant. Our imperial will is that the same should happen to all those of our subjects, whether of noble birth or not, who have in this way seized the land of the poor."

to heir and co-emperor with Michael III. In 867, Basil assassinated Michael to become sole emperor.

Basil I was good for the empire. Under him, the Byzantine state became almost as powerful as it had been under Justinian I. Constantinople had even more trade, more wealth, and more art than during Justinian's reign.

Byzantine prosperity was soon threatened by the struggle between Basil I's successors and the Powerful. In the tenth century, the great landholders gained control of much of the imperial army by grabbing up land in the military themes. Thus the very soldiers who had once given their loyalty to the emperor were now pledged to support the landlords. The Macedonian emperors could depend only on the troops they had stationed in and around Constantinople. These imperial troops spent a great deal of their time putting down revolts by the Powerful and their large private armies.

In 976 a teenage emperor, Basil II, came to the throne. When he grew older and acquired a mature understanding of the politics of the empire, this ruler, in

Empress Zoë appears before the people of Constantinople. Zoë ruled with her sister Theodora, and although the two did not always get along, together they were capable leaders, noted for their fairness and aptitude for eliminating corruption.

996, passed laws that hit hard at the Powerful, breaking up a number of the largest estates. However, after the death of Basil II in 1025, the landowners managed to have the laws repealed.

The Empresses Zoë and Theodora

Three years after Basil's death, the management of the empire fell to his nieces, Zoë and Theodora, daughters of the emperor Constantine VIII, who had been coruler with his brother Basil II. The two women could do nothing about the Powerful, but they handled other imperial affairs well. For instance, the empresses were judges in the highest imperial court, and their rulings were famed for their fairness.

Zoë and Theodora were particularly good at unearthing corrupt imperial officials. As historian Will Durant notes:

> Seldom had the Empire been better ruled. The imperial sisters attacked corruption in state and Church, and forced officials to disgorge [give up] their embezzled hoards; one . . . surrendered 5300 pounds of gold . . .; and when the [Constantinople] Patriarch Alexis died, a cache [stash] of 100,000 pounds of silver . . . was discovered in his rooms.[52]

The sisters' personal relations were not always so well managed. In 1042 Zoë became so jealous of her sister's power that she exiled Theodora to a convent. Thirteen years later, after Zoë's death, Theodora left the convent and ruled alone for the last year of her life.

The Church Divided

Near the end of Zoë and Theodora's rule, the fragile bond between the eastern and western churches broke permanently. The two churches were driven apart by conflict over doctrine. The Eastern Church believed that priests should be allowed to marry, the Roman Catholic Church did not. The Eastern Church taught that the Holy Spirit comes only from God, while Rome said that it arises from both God and Christ. Only the Eastern Church used leavened bread, which is baked with yeast to make it rise.

The fighting over these matters eventually went from words to actions. In 1052 news reached the patriarch of Constantinople, Michael Cerularius, that Pope Leo IX had forbidden the use of leavened bread in Byzantine churches in southern Italy. Cerularius, a former high government official, with a hard-nosed approach to matters, countered by closing western churches in Constantinople.

In 1054 a high-ranking Roman bishop, Cardinal Humbert, arrived in Constantinople to meet with Patriarch Cerularius. Humbert was "not the man to be cautious or subservient [submissive] in his negotiations."[53] Indeed, this short-tempered, unbending representative of the pope would accept only one response from the Eastern Church: it must give into the will of the Roman church. The patriarch, however, had no intention of submitting to the pope.

In the end the cardinal, enraged by his lack of success, excommunicated the patriarch, that is, banished him from the church, and stormed out of the Byzantine capital. Cerularius then excommunicated the cardinal, and the unity with the Catholic Church ended.

Defeat in Italy and Asia Minor

After Zoë and Theodora, the next several Byzantine rulers were a poor lot, unable to stop the growth of official corruption or check the Powerful. One result was the decline of the Byzantine military. The parts of the imperial army and navy not in the hands of the Powerful were reduced to skeleton forces, the money destined to buy equipment and to pay for soldiers and sailors going into the pockets of imperial officials.

Without an effective military, the empire was once more in peril. It lost its territory in Italy to the Normans, a group of invaders from northern France who began conquering Sicily and southern Italy in 1060. The Normans captured the last imperial Italian outpost, the seaport of Bari, in 1071.

The empire was also in trouble in the east. A new group of Muslims, the Seljuk Turks, had appeared in Asia Minor at about the same time as the Normans invaded Italy. In 1071 the Turks defeated an imperial army at Manzikert and captured the emperor, Romanos IV.

The Emperor Alexius I

In 1081 one of the Powerful seized the imperial throne, becoming Alexius I. The new emperor faced a situation almost as grim as that of Heraclius in the early

Conversion of the Russians

This account from the Russian Primary Chronicle, *excerpted from* The Eagle, the Crescent, and the Cross, *describes an event that occurred in 988: the conversion of a royal Russian, Prince Vladimir, to Byzantine Christianity.*

"The Greeks [Byzantines] sent to Vladimir a scholar. . . . [H]e exhibited to Vladimir a canvas [painting] on which was depicted the Judgment Day of the Lord, and showed him, on the right, the righteous going to . . . Paradise, and on the left, the sinners on their way to torment. Then Vladimir sighed and said, 'Happy are they upon the right, but woe [misery] to those upon the left!' The scholar replied, 'If you desire to take your place upon the right with the just, then accept baptism [initiation into the church]!' . . .

Vladimir summoned together his boyars [nobles] and the city-elders [of Kiev], and . . . they chose good and wise men to . . . go . . . among the Germans, and examine . . . [the faith of the Roman church], and finally to visit the Greeks. . . .

The [Byzantine] Emperor sent a message . . . to prepare the church and the clergy. . . . The Emperor accompanied the Russes [Russians] to the church . . ., calling their attention to the beauty of the edifice [building], the chanting, and the . . . services . . . and dismissed them with valuable presents and great honor.

Thus, they returned to their own country. . . . The envoys reported, . . . 'We went to . . . the Greeks . . ., and their service is fairer than the ceremonies of other nations.' . . . Vladimir then inquired where [in what place] they should all accept baptism."

Prince Vladimir of Russia (center) chose the Byzantine church over the Roman church when he accepted Christianity for himself and his nation in the late 900s.

seventh century. The Normans had not stopped advancing after throwing the Byzantines out of Italy but had crossed the Adriatic Sea to the imperial shores of the Balkans, and the Turks were still moving steadily across Asia Minor toward Constantinople. To counter these threats, Alexius I had only a government and army "crippled with treason, incompetence, corruption, and cowardice."[54]

Alexius I began by rebuilding the imperial army with money seized from the Byzantine church. Then in 1082 he persuaded the Italian city of Venice to agree to supply warships to be used against the Normans. In exchange for the ships, the emperor gave Venice trading rights in the empire. He also sent agents to Sicily to stir up trouble between the Italian population and their Norman overlords. In the end, the Normans were forced to retreat to the mainland of Italy.

Alexius I still had to deal with the Seljuk Turks, and again he sought help from the West. He proposed to the Roman church that eastern and western Christians combine forces and launch a holy war against the Muslim Turks. By bringing western Europeans into imperial affairs, Alexius set the stage for a disaster that would see the city of Constantinople fall for the first time to an attacking army.

Chapter

8 Crusaders and Latin Emperors

At the end of the eleventh century and continuing through the twelfth, thousands of western Europeans swarmed into the Byzantine Empire. They came at first to fight the Seljuk Turks and later to seek their fortunes through trade or service in the imperial government. Conflicts between these foreign adventurers and the Byzantines would come close to destroying the empire.

War Against the Turks

After their victory over the Byzantines at Manzikert, the Seljuk Turks continued advancing, overrunning more Byzantine territory in Asia Minor. They also defeated their fellow Muslims, the Arabs, winning control of the Near East, including Palestine and the city of Jerusalem, in 1087. By the 1090s, the Turks were the dominant force in the east.

The Byzantine emperor Alexius I needed help in fighting the Seljuks because the imperial army was not strong enough to handle the Turks alone. In 1095 the emperor sought aid from the Roman church, arguing that eastern and western Christians should join together in a holy war, or crusade, and push the non-Christian Seljuks out of Asia Minor.

The pope at the time, Urban II, agreed to cooperate with Alexius I and called for western Europeans to join the Byzantines in fighting the Turks. Urban hoped first that a joint East-West war against Muslims might reunite the western and eastern Christian churches. Second, the pope believed such a crusade could free not only Asia Minor but also Palestine and Jerusalem from Muslim rule.

To battle the Turks, Alexius I expected the West to send him a few hundred soldiers to fill out his army. What the First Crusade brought into the Byzantine Empire were several armies from France, Germany, and Italy, totaling some thirty thousand soldiers. There was no one in overall command of these western armies, which had been independently raised, each being led by a high-ranking noble—in one case, the brother of the French king. Below these commanders were lesser nobles, accompanied by their knights and foot soldiers.

The leaders of the European armies had their own plans and ambitions, which had little to do with those of Alexius I. The emperor wanted the lands in Asia Minor returned to the empire and, if possible, to make the Near East once more imperial territory. The western leaders wanted to enrich themselves on eastern loot and to carve out kingdoms.

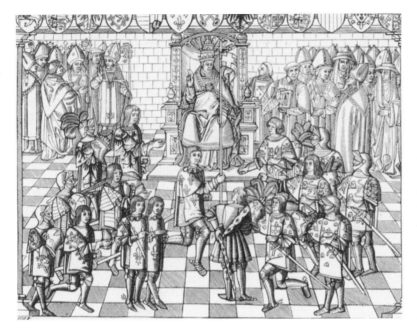

(Left) Pope Urban II calls for Roman and Byzantine Christians to unite, form the First Crusade, and take Palestine and Jerusalem back from the Muslim Turks. (Below) The crusaders (left) and the Turks (right) face off in the first battle of the First Crusade. The crusaders were victorious, taking Nicaea in Asia Minor from the Turks.

To safeguard his goals, Alexius required each of the crusade's leaders to swear an oath of loyalty to him. He hoped that this act would guarantee that any land in Asia Minor regained by the crusaders would be turned over to the empire and that any new states the westerners might create would be under imperial control. Obtaining these oaths was not always easy, and Alexius used everything from bribes to withholding food to force them out of the crusaders.

The Crusader States

The crusade won its first victory against the Turks in 1097 when it captured Nicaea, capital of Turkish Asia Minor. Alexius and the Byzantine army took part in this campaign, but later, while on his way to Antioch in Syria, the emperor heard rumors of a large Muslim force headed his way and retreated. The westerners, feeling betrayed, continued the war, moving successfully through Syria and into Palestine, where in 1099 they took Jerusalem.

The reconquered portions of Asia Minor were turned over to the Byzantines, while the victorious crusaders set up four

Near Eastern kingdoms. These crusader states were centered on the cities of Edessa, Antioch, Tripoli, and Jerusalem. Alexius I insisted that he had authority over these kingdoms, but he had little success in enforcing that authority.

During the twelfth century, the Muslims regrouped and began winning back their lost land. In 1144 they took Edessa, and in 1187, Jerusalem. All the remaining crusader kingdoms eventually fell to the Muslims.

The Muslim offensive sparked several other western crusading efforts. The Byzantines, however, had little to do with most of these ventures.

The Byzantines and the Latins

After the First Crusade, westerners, known to the Byzantines as Latins, were found all over the empire. The Latins did business in Constantinople and served in the imperial army. They even found positions in the government: During the twelfth-century reign of Emperor Manuel I, westerners held administrative and diplomatic posts.

The Byzantines and the Latins often disliked one another, and relations between the groups were generally strained. The Latins saw imperial citizens as soft, effeminate, and treacherous. The Byzantines, on the other hand, thought that the westerners were ill-mannered, savage barbarians and bitterly complained "of these foreigners, who . . . were ignorant of Greek culture and language."[55] Additionally, Byzantines and Latins looked on each other as religious heretics.

Amidst the turmoil of battle, a triumphant crusader enters Jerusalem in 1099 during the First Crusade. The western crusaders took Jerusalem without help from the Byzantines, who had retreated.

Adding to the friction between the Byzantines and the Latins was the empire's increasing dependence on trade with Venice. The trade alliance Alexius I had made with Venice gave the Venetians the right to import and export goods without paying customs duties. The merchants of Venice were also exempted from paying taxes and were given an entire section of Constantinople in which to locate homes, warehouses, and even churches.

Venice took over many of the empire's eastern and western trade routes, and as a result, the Byzantines lost control of their own trade during the first half of the twelfth century. Much of the profit that had once gone to imperial merchants and, through their taxes, into the imperial treasury, now went west to Venice. As the scholar Steven Runciman observes:

It was impossible for the people of Constantinople . . . not to resent these . . . westerners strutting through their streets . . . and enriching themselves at the expense of the local merchants; and when they brought their chaplains [clergymen] with them and were permitted to erect Latin churches, the anger increased.[56]

Massacre of the Latins

In 1171, to combat the power of the Venetians, Emperor Manuel I arrested ten

---

The Crusaders at Constantinople

In these two accounts from The Alexiad, *as quoted first in Harold Lamb's book,* The Crusades *and second in* Great Cities of the Ancient World, *Anna Comnena, daughter of Byzantine emperor Alexius I, describes her mixed feelings about Bohemund, a Norman officer with the First Crusade, and her shock at the rudeness of other western leaders.*

"Such a man had never been seen before in the lands of the Romans, for he was marvelous to the sight. . . . His clear blue eyes betokened [signaled] spirit and dignity. . . . A peculiar charm hung around this man, and yet there was something horrible in him. For in the size of his body and the glance of his eye . . . , he revealed power and savagery. Even his laughter sounded like snorting."

"Now the Frankish [western] Counts are naturally shameless and violent, naturally greedy of money too, and immoderate [excessive] in everything they wish . . . ; they did not make their visits [to the emperor] in any order. . . . [T]heir speech was very long-winded, and as they had no reverence [respect] for the Emperor, nor took heed of the lapse of time, . . . not one of them gave place to those who came after them, but kept on unceasingly with their talk and requests. . . . For even when evening came, the Emperor . . . rose from his throne to retire . . . , but not even then was he freed from the Franks' importunity [begging]. For one came after the other and not only those who had not been heard during the day, but the same [ones] came over again, always proferring one excuse after another for further talk."

thousand of the Europeans and seized their property. He then shipped his prisoners back to Venice, canceling the Venetians' trading rights.

However, many thousands of Latins remained in Constantinople, and Byzantine hatred of the westerners grew more intense over the next decade. In 1182 anti-Latin feelings were stirred to a fever pitch by the cousin of Emperor Alexius II, Andronicus Comnenus, who sent mobs of angry Byzantines swarming through Constantinople, killing any Latins they found. The final death toll was in the thousands. Andronicus, riding a wave of popularity at having bested the hated Latins, strangled Alexius II and took the throne as Andronicus I.

In 1185, in revenge for the massacre set in motion by Andronicus, Normans from Sicily plundered and murdered their way through Thessalonica, the second largest city in the empire. The news of Thessalonica's fate and the possibility of the Nor-

A Western View of the Byzantine

Western Europeans and the Byzantines did not get along because the two cultures were very different. This account, which reveals the western European prejudice against the Byzantines, is taken from the History of Deeds Done Beyond the Sea *by the historian William of Tyre and is quoted in* Byzantine Christianity: Emperor, Church, and the West, *by Harry J. Magoulias.*

"During the reign of Manuel [1143–1180] . . . , the Latins [western Europeans] had found great favor with him—a reward well deserved because of their loyalty and value. The emperor, a great-souled man of incomparable [matchless] energy, relied so implicitly [absolutely] on their fidelity and ability that he passed over the Greeks [Byzantines] as soft and effeminate and intrusted important affairs to the Latins alone. The Greek nobles . . . and the rest of the people as well, . . . conceived . . . [a] hatred toward us, and this was increased by the difference between our sacraments [religious rituals] and those of their church, which furnished an additional incentive to their jealousy. For they, having separated insolently from the church of Rome, in their boundless [vast] arrogance looked upon everyone who did not follow their foolish traditions as a heretic. It was they themselves . . . who deserved the name of heretics, because they had either created or followed new . . . beliefs contrary to the Roman church. . . . For these and other reasons they had for a long time cherished this hatred in their hearts and were ever seeking an opportunity . . . to destroy utterly the hated race of the Latins, both in the city and throughout the entire empire."

mans arriving at Constantinople sent a wave of panic through the Byzantine capital.

Like Alexius I, Andronicus had to turn to Venice for help in stopping the Normans. That help, as before, was paid for with trading rights within the empire, the same ones canceled in 1171. The emperor's move, however, did not satisfy the terrified citizens of Constantinople, and a mob attacked and killed Andronicus.

The Fourth Crusade

The hatred, fear, and violence climaxed twenty years later with the Fourth Crusade. The crusaders, although their goal was Jerusalem, had decided that their best strategy would be to take Egypt and then drive east and north into Palestine. Enrico Dandolo, the eighty-year-old doge (duke) of Venice, promised the crusaders both transport and warships. The asking price was steep.

Upon reaching Venice, the crusaders were approached by Alexius Angelus, nephew of Alexius III, the Byzantine emperor. The imperial nephew offered to pay the crusaders' debt to Venice if the Christian troops would help him become emperor.

Alexius's offer also suited the Venetians, who encouraged the crusaders to take it for two reasons. First, the Venetians had again been thrown out of the empire, and expected to regain their trading rights when Alexius was on the throne. Second, they had a secret treaty with Egypt that called for Venice to prevent any crusader invasion of the North African nation.

In the summer of 1203, the Fourth Crusade, accompanied by a large party of

Enrico Dandolo, the duke of Venice, makes his way to Constantinople during the Fourth Crusade. For a sizable fee, he provided the crusaders with the ships to take them to war and fend off enemies.

Venetians, landed at Constantinople and attacked the city. Using ladders, they scaled the walls and began setting fire to houses below. This action was enough to make Emperor Alexius III flee the city, taking a large part of the imperial treasury with him. The absent ruler's nephew now entered the city and declared himself emperor, taking the name Alexius IV, while outside the city walls the crusaders waited for their pay.

At first, the citizens of Constantinople accepted Alexius IV and his allies as just another set of characters in the ongoing drama of imperial Byzantine intrigue.

The crusaders' ships arrive in Constantinople in 1203. When the crusaders realized that the new emperor would not pay them the money Alexius IV had promised, they attacked. Constantinople surrendered, and was looted for three days.

However, when they learned of the new emperor's bargain with the crusaders, they were outraged. With the treasury emptied by Alexius III, huge tax increases would be necessary to pay off the Fourth Crusade. Alexius IV was strangled, and a new anti-Latin emperor took his place.

In the spring of 1204, when the crusaders realized that they were not going to be paid, they laid siege to Constantinople. No great general or able emperor stepped forward to direct the city's defenses, as had happened in the past. Moreover, the Byzantine army was at an all-time low, being in worse shape than it had been during the reign of Emperor Phocas six centuries before. The siege lasted a month, and then the city surrendered.

When Constantinople threw open its gates, the crusaders poured through them. The looting and destruction were enormous. As historian David Nicholas writes:

The crusaders . . . sacked it [Constantinople] for three days. The crusaders burned the entire city, including the imperial library and its irreplaceable manuscripts, carried off thousands of relics and smashed whatever statuary was too big to be easily portable. . . .

The sack of Constantinople was a cultural disaster. . . . Although some manuscripts were salvaged . . . , the fact that we have only tiny fragments of the original[s] . . . of Plato, Aristotle, the Greek dramatists and poets testifies to the thoroughness of the conflagration [fire].[57]

The Classics That Survived

Although it is true that the originals of many ancient Greek and Roman works were lost in the 1204 sack of Constantinople, copies of many of these classics did survive, and the copies were eventually brought to Italy by Byzantine teachers and scholars. As the scholar Will Durant notes:

[Byzantines] . . . brought Greek manuscripts to South Italy, and restored there a knowledge of Greek letters;

Greek [Byzantine] professors . . . left Constantinople, sometimes settled in Italy, and served as carriers of the classic germ; so year by year Italy rediscovered Greece, until men drank themselves drunk at the fountain of intellectual freedom.[58]

In addition to copies in Greek and Latin, others existed in Arabic. Muslim scholars, after visiting Constantinople, had translated a number of ancient classics into Arabic, and these were available to western Europeans in the libraries of Muslim Spain.

The victorious crusaders formed the Latin Empire and elected one of their own, Baldwin of Flanders, emperor. Venice carefully claimed for itself the

Smoke fills the air and the dead litter the ground as crusaders sack Constantinople. Much of the city's original Greek and Roman literature was also destroyed during the looting.

coastal towns and islands that would be the most valuable in conducting trade with the eastern Mediterranean.

The Latin Empire was a shaky venture from the start. In 1204 the Latin rulers controlled only Constantinople. They had almost no money. They were poor diplomats who were surrounded by a hostile Byzantine population and by many enemy states.

To the west and south were imperial lands that resisted the Latin Empire until conquered by it. To the north of the Latin Empire was the aggressive Bulgarian Empire, which attacked its new neighbor in 1205. During this war, the Latin emperor Baldwin was captured and killed.

The Empire of Nicaea

To the east was the Latin Empire's greatest foe, the empire of Nicaea. It was to Nicaea in western Asia Minor that many of the refugees from Constantinople fled. There, in 1205, Theodore Lascaris, a relative of the imperial family, established a Byzantine government in exile.

Unlike the Latin Empire, Nicaea had a strong government and a sound economy, modeled on the Byzantine Empire of Justinian I and Basil I. As the historian George Ostrogorsky relates:

Theodore Lascaris followed the pattern of old Byzantium in every detail. Administration, civil service and imperial household were revived. . . . The political and ecclesiastical [religious] traditions of the Byzantine Empire, . . . [represented by] . . . the Emperor and the Patriarch, were . . . renewed in Nicaea. . . . [The] appointed Patriarch

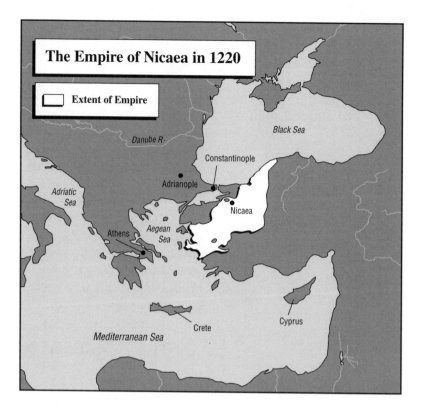

The Empire of Nicaea in 1220

Extent of Empire

Black Sea

Danube R.

Constantinople

Adrianople

Nicaea

Adriatic
Sea

Athens

Aegean
Sea

Crete

Cyprus

Mediterranean Sea

crowned Theodore Emperor. . . . He was now considered to be the sole legal Emperor of the Byzantines. . . . A Byzantine Emperor and an Orthodox Patriarch in Nicaea were now opposed to the Latin Emperor and Patriarch in Constantinople.[59]

In 1214 the Nicaean Empire declared war on the Latin Empire, but the conflict ended in stalemate. There matters stood for almost half a century. Then, in 1259, a new emperor, Michael VIII, won a major battle over the westerners.

Two years later, in July 1261, a small Byzantine army found Constantinople virtually undefended. At the time, the two empires had declared a temporary truce, and the Latin emperor and most of his troops were off besieging an island fortress in the Black Sea. Despite the truce, the Byzantines, supposedly on a scouting mission, promptly invaded and captured the capital. When the Latins in the Black Sea heard the news, they fled the region. Michael VIII entered Constantinople on August 15, thus ending the Latin Empire and restoring the Byzantine Empire.

The Ghost of an Empire

The emperors of the last two hundred years of Byzantium ruled over a ghost empire. The sack of Constantinople and almost sixty years of western rule so seriously damaged the empire that it never fully recovered. As historian David Nicholas observes:

> The emperors had less wealth and power than some powerful landed families . . . and had to use mercenary soldiers, who were expensive and unreliable. The Byzantine fleet had virtually ceased to exist, and the Empire relied on Italians . . . for transport and defense.[60]

The Shattered Empire

As Emperor Michael VIII and his troops rode into Constantinople on a summer day in 1261, they got their first good look at the Byzantine capital. Even a half century after the plundering and looting, the damage done to the city had only been partially repaired, and the city was still underpopulated.

As for the rest of the old empire, Michael was able to reconquer only fragments. Still, the Byzantine emperor did prevent a new western invasion that was being planned by Charles of Anjou, ruler of the Kingdom of the Two Sicilies. Michael engineered a revolt in Sicily that not only prevented the invasion but led to Charles's overthrow, as well.

Michael VIII also put an end to Venice's imperial trade monopoly by giving trading rights to another Italian city, Genoa. This action set off a fierce rivalry between the two cities, but despite the Byzantine emperor's hopes, it did not end Latin meddling in imperial affairs because "the Genoese and the Venetians, usually at war with each other, [still] interfered at every turn in the internal affairs of the Empire."[61]

The emperors who followed Michael VIII were no more successful than he in reconquering old imperial lands. Civil wars between rivals for the emperorship sapped the already badly drained empire of energy and resources. For those last two centuries, the imperial domain included little more than Constantinople and small portions of Asia Minor and the Balkans.

In the fourteenth century, a new group of Turks, the Ottomans, came out of Asia and swept across Asia Minor. In 1354 the Turks occupied Gallipoli, their first foothold in the empire's European territory. Nine years later, the Ottomans moved their capital from Asia Minor to Adrianople. From there, they quickly captured what little imperial land remained outside Constantinople. The emperors appealed to western Europe for help but received none.

The Fall of Constantinople

The Byzantine emperors managed to keep Constantinople out of Turkish hands for a few more decades by making bargains with the Ottomans. For instance, Emperor John V actually provided military assistance to the Turks during the last half of the fourteenth century. Finally, in 1453, the Ottomans moved on Constantinople. The Ottoman leader, Mehmet II, wanted to end this lone holdout against Turkish rule.

The Byzantine emperor was Constantine XI, who before mounting the throne in 1449 had fought well but uselessly against the Turks in Greece. Now, he did what little he could to prepare his city for the coming attack. Repeated requests for help from western Europe brought only a few volunteers. In the end, Constantine mustered 5,000 Byzantine soldiers plus another 3,000 westerners to meet Mehmet II and his 100,000 troops.

Even though the city had been captured twice before, it was difficult to defeat. Its walls remained strong, and its citizens and soldiers were ready for the Ottomans. For over a month, the Turks besieged the city with infantry, cannons, and ships. Finally, on May 29, 1453, Mehmet launched

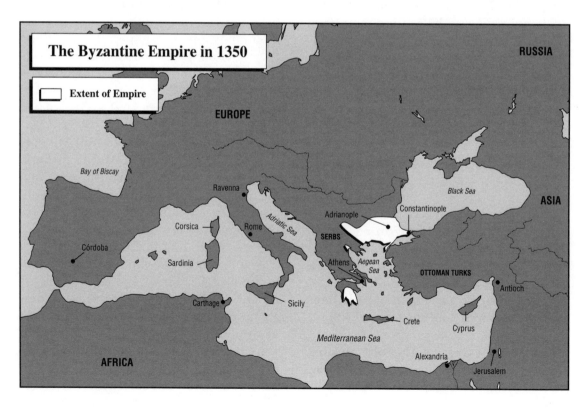

The Byzantine Empire in 1350

Extent of Empire

an all-out attack, the Turks hitting the city from three sides. The battle raged for hours, but finally, the Turks got enough ladders up against the city walls and enough soldiers into the city to turn the tide in their favor. Thousands were killed in the fighting, including Constantine XI.

After the Empire

After more than a thousand years, the Byzantine Empire was no more, its end, as its beginning, coming under the rule of an Emperor Constantine. Yet, the influence of Byzantium did not die with the empire. That influence was felt by the Turks, who now controlled the same lands long ruled by the Byzantines. The Ottomans created their own empire, using the Byzantine model, with Constantinople, now dubbed Istanbul, their capital.

In other parts of Europe, the Byzantine Empire also left its mark, providing the ancient Greek and Roman foundation on which the western world rests. As the historian George Ostrogorsky concludes:

> The Byzantine state was the instrument by . . . which . . . Graeco-Roman antiquity survived through the ages, and . . . Byzantium was the donor, the West the recipient. This was particularly true at the time of the renaissance, when there was such passionate interest in classical civilization and the West found that it could satisfy its longings to explore the treasures of antiquity from Byzantine sources. Byzantium . . . had saved from destruction Roman law, Greek literature, philosophy and learning, so that this . . . heritage could be passed on to the people of western Europe who were now ready to receive it.[62]

Notes

Introduction: The Legacy of Empire

1. Will Durant, *The Story of Civilization*, Vol. 4, *The Age of Faith*. New York: Simon & Schuster, 1950.
2. George Ostrogorsky, *History of the Byzantine State*, rev. ed. Translated by Joan Hussey. New Brunswick, NJ: Rutgers University Press, 1969.
3. Ostrogorsky, *History of the Byzantine State*.
4. Durant, *The Age of Faith*.

Chapter 1: From Rome to Byzantium

5. Durant, *The Age of Faith*.
6. David Nicholas, *The Evolution of the Medieval World: Society, Government and Thought in Europe, 312–1500*. London: Longman Group, 1992.
7. L. Sprague de Camp, *Great Cities of the Ancient World*. Garden City, NY: Doubleday, 1972.
8. Crane Brinton et al., *A History of Civilization*, Vol. 1, *Prehistory to 1715*, 2nd ed. Englewood Cliffs, NJ: Prentice-Hall, 1960.
9. Durant, *The Age of Faith*.
10. Durant, *The Age of Faith*.
11. Norman F. Cantor, *The Civilization of the Middle Ages*. New York: HarperCollins, 1993.

Chapter 2: Byzantine Society

12. Steven Runciman, *Byzantine Civilization*. New York: Barnes & Noble, 1933.
13. Brinton, *A History of Civilization*.
14. Quoted in Charles Diehl, *Byzantine Empresses*. Translated by Harold Bell and Theresa de Kerpely. London: Elek Books, 1927.
15. Harold Lamb, *The Crusades*. Garden City, NY: Doubleday, 1945.
16. Runciman, *Byzantine Civilization*.
17. Durant, *The Age of Faith*.

18. Tamara Talbot Rice, *Everyday Life in Byzantium*. New York: Barnes & Noble, 1967.
19. Rice, *Everyday Life in Byzantium*.

Chapter 3: Byzantine Christianity

20. Brinton, *A History of Civilization*.
21. Runciman, *Byzantine Civilization*.
22. Quoted in Rice, *Everyday Life in Byzantium*.
23. Nicholas, *The Evolution of the Medieval World*.
24. Runciman, *Byzantine Civilization*.
25. Aikaterina Christophilopoulou, *Byzantine History*, Vol. 1, *324–610*. Translated by W. W. Phelps. Amsterdam: Adolf M. Hakkert, 1986.
26. Steven Runciman, *The Byzantine Theocracy*. Cambridge, Cambridge University Press, 1977.
27. Ostrogorsky, *History of the Byzantine State*.

Chapter 4: Byzantine Culture

28. Brinton, *A History of Civilization*.
29. Durant, *The Age of Faith*.
30. Nicholas, *The Evolution of the Medieval World*.
31. Rice, *Everyday Life in Byzantium*.
32. In *Ecclesiastical History*. Quoted in Durant, *The Age of Faith*.
33. Runciman, *Byzantine Civilization*.
34. de Camp, *Great Cities of the Ancient World*.
35. Quoted in Brinton, *A History of Civilization*.

Chapter 5: Riots, Laws, and Conquest

36. *Secret History*. Translated by Richard Atwater. Ann Arbor: University of Michigan Press, 1961.
37. Durant, *The Age of Faith*.
38. Quoted in Christophilopoulou, *Byzantine History*.

39. In *History of the Wars*. Quoted in Brinton, *A History of Civilization*.

40. Justinian, *The Civil Law*. Translated by S. P. Scott. Quoted in Charles T. Davis, ed., *The Eagle, the Crescent, and the Cross: Sources of Medieval History, Vol. I (c. 250–c. 1000)*. New York: Appleton-Century-Crofts, 1967.

41. Christophilopoulou, *Byzantine History*.

42. Robert Browning, *Justinian and Theodora*, rev. ed. London: Thames & Hudson, 1987.

43. In *History of the Wars*. Quoted in Durant, *The Age of Faith*.

Chapter 6: Slavs, Avars, Persians, and Muslims

44. Ostrogorsky, *History of the Byzantine State*.

45. Durant, *The Age of Faith*.

46. Brinton, *A History of Civilization*.

47. Ostrogorsky, *History of the Byzantine State*.

48. Durant, *The Age of Faith*.

49. Ostrogorsky, *History of the Byzantine State*.

Chapter 7: Bulgars, Heretics, and Landlords

50. Ostrogorsky, *History of the Byzantine State*.

51. Runciman, *Byzantine Civilization*.

52. Durant, *The Age of Faith*.

53. Cantor, *The Civilization of the Middle Ages*.

54. Durant, *The Age of Faith*.

Chapter 8: Crusaders and Latin Emperors

55. Harry J. Magoulias, *Byzantine Christianity: Emperor, Church and the West*. Detroit: Wayne State University Press, 1970.

56. Runciman, *The Byzantine Theocracy*.

57. Nicholas, *The Evolution of the Medieval World*.

58. Durant, *The Age of Faith*.

59. Ostrogorsky, *History of the Byzantine State*.

Conclusion: The Ghost of an Empire

60. Nicholas, *The Evolution of the Medieval World*.

61. Brinton, *A History of Civilization*.

62. Ostrogorsky, *History of the Byzantine State*.

For Further Reading

After Jesus: The Triumph of Christianity. New York: Reader's Digest/Random House, 1992. A solid, readable history of the stormy struggle that created church organization and doctrines. Text is supplemented with a glossary, a bibliography, maps, and many color photos of art work.

Timothy L. Biel, *The Crusades.* San Diego, CA: Lucent Books, 1995. Traces the history of the crusades, looking at the interactions of the societies that gave birth to them. Black-and-white illustrations, excerpts from eyewitness accounts, maps, a time line, and additional reading enhance the text.

James A. Corrick, *The Early Middle Ages* and *The Late Middle Ages.* Both: San Diego, CA: Lucent Books, 1995. Filled with instructive illustrations, these two books trace the history of Europe from the fall of Rome to the beginning of the Renaissance. They also contain excerpts from period documents, maps, a time line, and a reading list.

John Dunn, *The Spread of Islam.* San Diego, CA: Lucent Books, 1996. A well-illustrated introduction to the history of Islam, its origins and growth. Text is supplemented with excerpts from Arabic and European manuscripts, a time line, a reading list, and maps.

Harold Lamb, *Theodora and the Emperor: The Drama of Justinian.* Garden City, NY: Doubleday, 1952. Reading almost like a novel, this biography of the emperor Justinian I and his wife, Theodora, is filled with interesting facts about the two, their lives, and the politics of the time.

John S. Major, *The Silk Route.* New York: HarperCollins, 1994. Follows an imaginary caravan carrying silk from China to Constantinople in A.D. 700. Describes the farming of silkworms, the dangers of the trail, the tactics of Byzantine merchants, and the importance of the cloth to the Byzantine world. A map of the route and color illustrations accompany the text.

Don Nardo, *The Roman Empire.* San Diego, CA: Lucent Books, 1994. A solid introduction to the history of the Roman Empire; covers the creation of the eastern Roman Empire, the early centuries of Christianity, and the barbarian invasions. In addition to the text, there are many illustrations, excerpts from Roman documents, maps, a time line, and a reading list.

Ewart O. Oakeshott, *Dark Age Warrior.* Chester Springs, PA: Dufour, 1984. This good, readable history of the migration of the early Germanic peoples goes into tribal religion, organization, and life. Text is supported by detailed line drawings.

Jill Paton Walsh, *The Emperor's Winding Sheet.* New York: Farrar, Straus, and Giroux, 1974. A well-researched novel about the siege and fall of Constantinople in 1453. The events and people are seen through the eyes of a young servant to Emperor Constantine XI.

Works Consulted

Crane Brinton, John B. Christopher, and Robert Lee Wolff, *A History of Civilization*, Vol. 1, *Prehistory to 1715*, 2nd ed. Englewood Cliffs, NJ: Prentice-Hall, 1960. The chapters on the Byzantine Empire give a good, clear outline, as well as presenting a balanced account, of the internal and external struggles of the empire.

Robert Browning, *Justinian and Theodora*, rev. ed. London: Thames & Hudson, 1987. An in-depth study of the age of Justinian. Sketches in the character of the important people of the time, and looks in detail at the emperor's policies, legal reform, wars, and building programs. Some thirty black-and-white photographs show examples of the art and architecture of the period. A table of dates and a reading list are included.

Norman F. Cantor, *The Civilization of the Middle Ages*. New York: HarperCollins, 1993. A thorough, updated history of the Middle Ages by an eminent medieval scholar. In addition to facts, the book provides insights into the people and events important to Byzantine history.

Aikaterina Christophilopoulou, *Byzantine History*, Vol. 1, *324–610*. Translated by W. W. Phelps. Amsterdam: Adolf M. Hakkert, 1986. A thorough study by an eminent Greek historian of the first three centuries of the Byzantine Empire from the founding of Constantinople to the reign of the emperor Heraclius.

Charles T. Davis, ed., *The Eagle, the Crescent, and the Cross: Sources of Medieval History*, Vol. I (*c. 250–c. 1000*). New York: Appleton-Century-Crofts, 1967. An excellent source of Byzantine writings. Each Byzantine piece is either by or about a major imperial figure.

L. Sprague de Camp, *Great Cities of the Ancient World*. Garden City, NY: Doubleday, 1972. The chapter on Constantinople is full of interesting information about the history and growth of the city from the time of Constantine I to the modern day. Photographs and maps complement the text.

Charles Diehl, *Byzantine Empresses*. Translated by Harold Bell and Theresa de Kerpely. London: Elek Books, 1927. A very readable account of the lives and political careers of fourteen Byzantine empresses.

Will Durant, *The Story of Civilization*, Vol. 4, *The Age of Faith*. New York: Simon & Schuster, 1950. A classic study of the Middle Ages that is written in a readable and accessible style and ends with a large bibliography. Its sections on the Byzantine Empire are filled with facts, incidents, and speculation about the culture.

The History of Menander the Guardsman. Translated by R. C. Blockley. Liverpool: Francis Cairns, 1985. An account of the years following the death of Justinian I by the contemporary historian Menander. Provides much information on imperial politics and Byzantine relations with Persia and the Avars.

C. Warren Hollister et al., eds., *Medieval Europe: A Short Sourcebook*. New York: John Wiley, 1982. A useful, if limited, collection, containing a few original Byzantine writings, some of which are modern translations.

Walter Emil Kaegi Jr., *Army, Society and Religion in Byzantium*. London: Variorum Reprints, 1982. A collection of articles examining tactics, equipment, morale, and leadership in the Byzantine army.

Kassia: The Legend, the Woman and Her Work. Edited and translated by Antonia Tripolitis. New York: Garland Publishing, 1992. A collection of the religious poetry and hymns of the ninth-century Byzantine poet Kassia.

Harold Lamb, *The Crusades*. Garden City, NY: Doubleday, 1945. A very readable and informative history of the crusades. Half the book deals with the First Crusade, presenting a balanced account of the interactions of the Byzantines and the crusaders.

Harry J. Magoulias, *Byzantine Christianity: Emperor, Church and the West*. Detroit: Wayne State University Press, 1970. A scholarly study of the nature of the Eastern Church and its importance to the development and political aims of the Byzantine Empire.

David Nicholas, *The Evolution of the Medieval World: Society, Government and Thought in Europe, 312–1500*. London: Longman Group, 1992. An excellent history of the Middle Ages with sections on the Byzantine Empire that show how religion, politics, art, and everyday life contributed to the development of the empire. Each chapter ends with a list of suggested readings, and the book has an excellent map section.

Nikephoros, Patriarch of Constantinople: Short History. Translated by Cyril Mango. Washington, DC: Dumbarton Oaks, 1990. An account by the ninth-century Byzantine churchman Nikephoros detailing the reigns of Heraclius and several of the emperors who succeeded him. Provides much interesting information about the final Persian war.

George Ostrogorsky, *History of the Byzantine State*, rev. ed. Translated by Joan Hussey. New Brunswick, NJ: Rutgers University Press, 1969. A revision of a classic study of the Byzantine Empire by a famous historian. Maps out the complex events that took the empire from the time of Constantine I to that of Constantine XI. Many full color maps depict the various gains and losses of the empire.

Procopius, *Secret History*. Translated by Richard Atwater. Ann Arbor: University of Michigan Press, 1961. This famous Byzantine historian's exposé of Emperor Justinian I and the Empress Theodora.

Tamara Talbot Rice, *Everyday Life in Byzantium*. New York: Barnes & Noble, 1967. Full of black-and-white drawings that support descriptions of all aspects of Byzantine life, covering such topics as the emperor and his family, the church, the army and navy, town and country life, and artists and architects. Has a reading list and a chronology of the emperors.

David Ricks, *Byzantine Heroic Poetry*. Bristol: Bristol Classical Press, 1990. A translation of the *Digenes Akrites*, the most famous Byzantine epic poem.

The Roman History of Ammianus Marcellinus. Translated by C. D. Yonge, London:

G. Bell and Sons, 1911. Packed with information, much of it firsthand, about the fourth-century eastern and western Roman empires. Vivid and colorful accounts of military life and battles such as Adrianople, as well as informative descriptions of various barbarians from the Visigoths to the Huns.

Steven Runciman, *Byzantine Civilization*. New York: Barnes & Noble, 1933. A classic study by a well-known historian. After a brief outline of Byzantine history, each chapter looks at a different part of Byzantine culture and society, ending with a discussion of the empire's relations with neighboring states.

————, *The Byzantine Theocracy*. Cambridge: Cambridge University Press, 1977. In a clear, readable style, traces the religious history of the Byzantine Empire.

Examines the role of monks and priests in the empire's society and presents easy-to-follow explanations of the various heresies and religious doctrines of the Byzantine church.

J. Stevenson, *Creeds, Councils, and Controversies: Documents Illustrating the History of the Church, AD 337–461*. Revised by W. H. C. Frend. London: Society for the Preservation of Christian Knowledge, 1989. A good collection of excerpts from early church writings covering such subjects as the relation of the church to the empire, Monophysitism, and the pope's supremacy.

Three Byzantine Saints: Contemporary Biographies. Translated by Elizabeth Dawes and Norman H. Baynes. London: Mowbrays, 1948. Translations of accounts of the lives of three popular Byzantine saints.

Index

Jews, 46, 75
paganism, 39, 45–46, 49
persecution of heretics,
    pagans, and Jews, 45–46, 50
writings on, 51–52
see also Christianity; Islam
revolts and riots, 28, 80
  in Constantinople, 71
    Nika, 58–59
  massacre of Latins, 92
Robber Council, 45
Roman Catholic Church
  agrees to crusade against
    Turks, 88
  Croatia and, 79
  relations with Byzantine
    Church, 42–43, 45
  separates from Byzantine
    Church, 85
Roman Empire, 14–21, 23
  ancient
    influence of, on Byzantine
      culture, 45–48
    religion of, 45–46
  armies of, 17
  divided, 15–17
  eastern, 15–16, 21, 23
    barbarian invasions
      threaten, 18, 20
    extent of, 16
    Germanic peoples settle in,
      17, 19
    see also Byzantine Empire
  fall of, 10, 12, 21, 23, 66, 68
  influence of, on Byzantine
    law, 59, 60
  western, 15–17
    extent of, 16
    fall of, 10, 12, 21, 23, 66, 68
    Germanic peoples
      invade, 18–20
      rule, 21, 23
Rome

captured by Byzantines, 66, 68
captured by Visigoths, 18
see also Roman Empire
Romulus Augustulus (emperor),
  10, 21
Russia, 79, 86

sacrum consistorium (cabinet), 26
saints, 52
Santa Sophia, Church of, 53, 54
senate, Byzantine, 26, 28
Seljuk Turks, 85
  First Crusade against, 87–90
Serbia, 79–80
serfs, 34
  Code of Justinian and, 61
slaves, 34–35
  Code of Justinian and, 61
Slavs, 77–80
  attack Byzantine Empire,
    70–71
  settle in the Balkans, 77
society, 32–37
Spain
  conquered by Arabs, 76
  occupied by Byzantine, 66, 68
stylites, 41, 52
Symeon, 78–79
Syria, 71, 89
  see also Antioch, Syria; Near
    East

taxes, 24, 32, 35, 70
  Muslim, on nonbelievers, 75
  under Justinian I, 63
themes (military districts), 73–74
Theodora (empress, sister of
  Zoë), 84–85
Theodora (empress, wife of
  Justinian I), 56–59
Theodore Lascaris (emperor),
  95–96
Theodoric the Great, 23

Thessalonica, Greece
  sacked by Normans, 92–93
trade, 11, 87, 90–92, 93, 97
treaties
  with Persian Empire, 65, 73
Tribonian (lawyer), 60, 64
Turks. *See* Ottoman Turks;
  Seljuk Turks

Valens (emperor), 15, 18, 19
Valentinian I (emperor),
  15–16
Venice, Italy, 95
  trade alliance with Byzantine
    Empire, 87, 90–92, 93, 97
Visigoths, 76
  invade Roman Empire, 18–20

wars, 63
  Crusades, 87–90, 93–94
  in North Africa, 65
  invasion of Italy, 65–68
  with Arabs, 74–76
  with barbarians, 70–71, 72, 74
  with Bulgarian Kingdom,
    77–78
  with Normans, 85, 87
  with Persian Empire, 65,
    71–72, 74
western Europe
  conflict between Byzantine
    Empire and, 90–94
  First Crusade and, 88–90
  massacre of Latins, 92
  protected by Byzantine
    Empire, 12–13, 76
women, and Byzantine law, 62

Yugoslavia, 79–80

Zeno (emperor)
  attempts to reunify Roman
    Empire, 21, 23

Picture Credits

Cover photo: Bettmann

Archive Photos, 12, 13, 17, 21, 31, 46, 54, 56, 62, 66, 72 (top), 80, 89 (both), 90, 93, 95

Archive Photos/Popperfoto, 11

The Bettmann Archive, 29

Corbis-Bettmann, 26, 33, 35, 38, 49 (top), 57, 58, 60, 69

Laurie Platt Winfrey, Inc., 55

Laurie Platt Winfrey, Inc./The J. Paul Getty Museum, 40

Laurie Platt Winfrey, Inc./Louvre, 74

North Wind Picture Archives, 18, 22, 48, 49 (bottom), 67, 68, 86

Stock Montage, Inc., 15, 25, 30, 36, 41, 42, 43, 44, 50, 53, 61, 65, 71, 72 (bottom), 79, 81, 84, 94

About the Author

James A. Corrick has been a professional writer and editor for more than fifteen years and is the author of twenty books, as well as two hundred articles and short stories. Other books for Lucent are *The Early Middle Ages, The Late Middle Ages,* and *The Battle of Gettysburg.* Along with a Ph.D. in English, Corrick's academic background includes a graduate degree in the biological sciences. He has taught English, tutored minority students, edited magazines for the National Space Society, been a science writer for the Muscular Dystrophy Association, and edited and indexed books on history, economics, and literature for Columbia University Press, MIT Press, and others. He lives in Tucson, Arizona, and, when not writing, reads, swims, walks, frequents bookstores, and holds forth on any number of topics. He is a member of the Arizona Historical Society and is on the board of directors of the Tucson Book Publishing Association.